1 MONTH OF
FREE
READING

at

www.ForgottenBooks.com

By purchasing this book you are eligible for one month membership to ForgottenBooks.com, giving you unlimited access to our entire collection of over 700,000 titles via our web site and mobile apps.

To claim your free month visit:

www.forgottenbooks.com/free139107

ISBN 978-0-260-91723-2
PIBN 10139107

MR. WILLIAM DAWSON.

WILLIAM DAWSON:

The 'Yorkshire Farmer' and

Eloquent Preacher.

BY

ANNE E. KEELING,

Author of 'John Nelson, Mason and Missionary,' 'Eminent Methodist Women,' etc., etc.

London:

CHARLES H. KELLY, 2, Castle St., City Rd., E.C.;

AND 66, PATERNOSTER ROW, E.C.

1894.

HE HELD HIMSELF A LITTLE ALOOF FROM HIS TRAVELLING COMPANIONS. —*p.* 75.

CONTENTS.

WILLIAM DAWSON:

THE YORKSHIRE FARMER AND ELOQUENT PREACHER.

CHAPTER I.

EARLY YEARS

HE WAS STANDING MUSING BY THE HEDGE-SIDE IN UTTER WRETCHEDNESS.—*p.* 11.

'HE was never called *Billy* at home, and I cannot conceive why he should be so distinguished abroad,' said the widowed mother of William Dawson, who fancied there was something of contempt in the familiar nickname by which her faithful, devoted son was most widely known. But the name had no such meaning on the lips of many good old Methodists, who could remember Dawson in his prime, whose eyes would sparkle and their speech grow eloquent, while they recalled 'Billy's' appearance and conversation and impressive pulpit ministrations. For them it **was** a title of affectionate **and** not of contemptuous familiarity, **and** its homeliness **was but** a tribute to the sturdy simplicity which delighted them in this famous Local Preacher.

The number of these veterans is daily growing fewer, and their stores of racy reminiscences are being lost to the new generation ; it seems well, then, that some fresh effort should be made to fix, before its colours can vanish, the image that glowed so vividly in their memories and in their talk—the image of a man perilously gifted and popular, whose lowliness of heart was proof against the temptations to which the successful preacher is all the more exposed when, like Dawson, he is self-taught and self-made; and who could quietly renounce, at the bidding of home duties and affections, the seemingly higher career to which both his tastes, his powers, and his influential friends all invited him ; being content to work with head and hands to support widowed mother and helpless brother, while devoting every moment of rightful leisure to that work of publishing the glorious Gospel, on which he would gladly have spent the whole of his time and ability, had it seemed to him that he was free so to consecrate himself. Such a character, such a life, are surely well worth our study.

William Dawson was born on the 30th of March, 1773, 'at Garforth, a small parish town, three miles from Aberford, and seven from Leeds, in the county of York.'* His father, Luke Dawson, acted as colliery agent to Sir Thomas Gascoigne, of Gawthorpe, from whom he rented a farm. A similar position of trust had been held by William's grandfather, colliery agent to Lord Irvine, of Temple Newsome,

* Everett's *Life of William Dawson.*

and by one of his granduncles, land and colliery agent to Sir Rowland Winn, of Nostell Priory. In social standing, therefore, Dawson's family was probably a grade higher than that of John Nelson, the Birstall stone-mason expert in his father's craft; yet the same character of uprightness and efficiency, the same faithful thoroughness in service, seem to have been common to both.

Luke Dawson stands before us in faint but clear outline, a man of strong sense though feeble constitution, single-hearted, steadfast, content to do good work for small pay.

'Neither my father nor myself,' said William in later life, 'were equally remunerated for our time and pains as agents of Sir Thomas Gascoigne. My father never had more than twelve shillings per week, and coals and candles allowed. I had twelve shillings per week till 1793, when the wages of the colliers were raised, and then I had fifteen shillings. The colliers struck again, about a year or two after this, when another advance took place, and my wages were raised to eighteen shillings per week. Thus, my father and myself served the Gascoigne family for a period of nearly forty years, for what I have stated.'

It would be small matter for wonder that the colliers 'struck,' if their earnings were as small in proportion to their work as those of the agent. Luke Dawson, however, did not 'strike,' and apparently did not complain, retaining his poorly-paid office to his life's end, and so discharging it as to earn the entire confidence of his employer.

'I shall not decide till I have first seen Luke Dawson, and consulted him on the subject,' Sir Thomas Gascoigne is reported to have said, when appealed to about matters on which he himself was quite competent to pronounce finally; and the words are eloquent as to the proved value of the agent. We have to remind ourselves that the comparative worth and purchasing power of money was much higher in that day than in our own, before we can reconcile ourselves to this employer for the poor recompense he thought sufficient for the services of such a man.

Luke Dawson died about the year 1791, having lived fifty years, of which twenty-one had been spent in the employ of Sir Thomas Gascoigne. Anne, his wife, whose maiden name was Pease, long outlived him, dying in 1824, when in the seventy-sixth year of her age. Her influence on her son William, the eldest of her ten children, was great and salutary. She joined deep, true piety to unusual force of character, and would seem to have been one of those grand old English matrons who are not the least among the glories of our family chronicles in this land. Her great shrewdness in business matters was reinforced by the rarer gift of intuition ; she could catch and interpret the subtle shifting meanings of brow and eye and lip, and read therein the hidden matters of the heart ; she could gather true impressions from the slightest indications of fact, and was weatherwise in the signs of coming changes in human affairs. Something of this special faculty she may have transmitted to her son, who, however imperfectly trained in the learning of the schools, knew well the hearts of men, and could play on them as on a familiar instrument.

The high, unbending integrity, the deep, reverent religion, which were hers as they had been her husband's, were a yet more precious heritage to William from both his parents

A delicate, sickly, fretful infant was little 'Willy' Dawson ; no one, in the first six months of his life, would have prophesied the stalwart manhood of his prime ; and not a member of the household, save one only, but was weary of the wailing baby ; even his father would say that it would be well if heaven released the child from its suffering existence. But the mother, whose rest was broken every night by the piteous whimperings and cries of her first-born, could never join in the wish; and it was to her patient love that he owed the care which preserved him for long years of hallowed usefulness. Here, then, we have another proof of the unwisdom and shortsightedness of that ancient Spartan legislation, which modern Socialism fain would imitate, that condemned to extinction every baby existence deficient in the promise of vigorous future health.

Dawson himself, with some humour, would attribute to the continual crying of his babyhood the remarkable lung-power he developed in after years.

Before his feeble little son could walk, Luke Dawson removed from Garforth to Barnbow—no great distance—where a house was in process of erection for him. Baby William's health was not to be risked in a new half-finished dwelling, therefore he was consigned to the care of his grandfather Dawson at Whitkirle; and here he spent five happy years, finding a playground quite to his mind in the parish churchyard that adjoined old Mr. Dawson's house. Here, among the rank churchyard grass, and the 'cold *Hic Jacets* of the dead,' gray tombs and humbler half-worn gravestones, he played with a beloved little comrade called William Arthur. Did *they* read the epitaphs and wonder ' where all the bad people were buried'? Little Dawson had been well enough taught for such studyings and won-derings, as an anecdote of this time witnesses. The two playfellows strayed into the church one day, the sexton having left the door open awhile; and there, it would seem, they were found, having 'a game at parson and clerk'; little Dawson occupying the pulpit, little Arthur the reading-desk, while the former read aloud ' a chapter,' in the proper clerical style, with sonorous voice and suitable emphasis;

struggling bravely with the ponderous covers of the parish
Bible, almost too heavy for him to open, and contriving, by
the help of a friendly hassock, to make himself tall enough
to be visible over the pulpit cushion, and to keep an eye on
his admiring 'clerk.' How dear such impersonations are to
church- and chapel-going little people, many a mother well
knows ; it was only Dawson's subsequent eminence that
made *his* mother dwell fondly on the little scene, and say,
' He was born a preacher.'

That the child was of a very loving nature, and, when
love bade, very resolute, appears touchingly in another
anecdote of this period. Little William Arthur sickened of
the dreaded small-pox, and his playfellow, as was right, was
strictly kept away from him. But Willy Dawson contrived
to escape unobserved from his own home, to steal unobserved into his friend's, and went soft-footed up the stair
to the darkened sick-chamber where the sufferer lay, fevered
and wretched, and, as it chanced, alone. Here the two
were found, clasped in each other's arms, the one who was
whole comforting the one that was sick with every device of
childish affection at his command. He was carried back to
his grandfather's, to sicken and suffer in his turn, as the
penalty of his disobedient lovingness. Happily the disease
was of no very malignant type ; both the boys recovered in
due course, and could play together as before, healthy and
unblemished ; and what might have been a pathetic child-
tragedy is only remembered as a significant incident in the
life of a noted Christian evangelist, whose 'yearning pity' for
the souls of men was nobly accompanied by 'piety at home.'

.Nearly five years were passed under the kind grandfather's roof, and those years of wholesome rustic freedom
developed the feeble infant into a sturdy boy, full of life and
vigour, who thoroughly enjoyed existence. ' Child, thou

hast a crop for all kinds of corn,' his grandmother was wont to say with blunt fondness. She spoke more truly than she knew. It was an eager enquiring spirit, with strong intellectual appetites, that looked out of the sparkling eyes of the rosy boy she loved.

Old Mr. Dawson died before his grandson had fulfilled his seventh year; and then the child was returned to the care of his own parents, and came fully under the strong religious influence of his mother. There were now other little ones in the home at Barnbow, and there were to be more. Altogether, ten boys and girls were born to Luke Dawson and his wife; four of these died in infancy, but six lived to be men and women. But amid all the busy cares that beset the hard-working mother of this little flock, she was daily and hourly mindful of their spiritual welfare; she always found time to pray with them, and to read to them from her Bible, and from the old-fashioned books that formed her theological library, especially from the *Practice of Piety*. Could this book be identical with that which John Bunyan's first wife brought to him as part of her humble dowry? It is not quite impossible, but the likelihood is for some later work under the much-esteemed old title. Drelincourt *On Death*, Flavel *On the Soul*, and some obscurer volume solemnly enforcing the paramount importance of religious decision, were among the books in Mrs. Dawson's possession that her son studied under her direction, and that had a distinct effect upon him. But it was the mother's teaching, much more than that of her favourite authors—it was her fervour in dwelling on the truths they set forth, which gave those truths their early power on the mind of William Dawson. ' I owe much to my mother!' he would repeat with intense emphasis in later life; and heartily would he have subscribed to the saying :

' Mighty is the force of motherhood ! '

The mother's teaching had more power in its simplicity than that of the good clergyman, Miles Atkinson, whose Evangelical ministry the Dawsons preferred to attend, though three miles lay between their home at Barnbow and his church at Kippax. Willy Dawson listened uncomprehendingly during four years to this pious man's discourses, and, for lack of understanding their phraseology, derived no benefit at all. It was otherwise when Mr. Atkinson was succeeded by the Rev. W. Richardson, who would seem to have preached with something of the directness, the quaintness, the boldness of a Latimer, and thus caught the ear and the fancy of the boy, now approaching his tenth year. He adopted as his own one of Mr. Richardson's peculiar terms, and would in his later pulpit ministrations speak of ' one-eyed Christians '—meaning thereby such as had ' the single eye '—an expression more noticeable for oddity than aptness. It is said, however, that Mr. Dawson succeeded in using it with good effect, not rarely.

William Dawson was less fortunate in the instructors to whom the secular part of his education was intrusted. His first schoolmaster, who held sway in a house close to Barwick churchyard, is described as incompetent, but amusingly pedantic—a worthy rival of the neighbouring pedagogue of Scoles, who, said Dawson, conscientiously read his Leeds newspaper daily, from end to end, without the omission of a word, and preferred to say that unknown facts would be ' developed,' instead of being merely ' brought to light.' From the word-monger of Barwick school William was transferred to the care of a reverend gentleman who took pupils in the same neighbourhood, but whose conduct was not such as suited his profession ; and - the boy's anxious parents found a second removal necessary.

This time he fell into good hands; and under the tuition of ' Mr. Ephraim Sanderson of Aberford,' who conducted a large day and boarding-school there, the youth made rapid progress, completing at this school the brief term of education which was thought necessary for one of his social standing in those days. Mr. Sanderson earned and kept the respect of his pupil by a happy union of ability, integrity, and good judgment ; the lively lad, with his perilously quick sense of humour, his keen eye for inconsistency, found nothing in *him* to ridicule or to contemn.

William was strongly influenced for good, when nearing his thirteenth year, by the Rev. Thomas Dikes, afterwards of Hull, but then curate of Barwick-in-Elmet. This gentleman took much notice of him, talked to him, wrote to him, and lent him useful books. None impressed him so much as Doddridge's *Rise and Progress of Religion in the Soul.* Over this book he would sit solitary in his father's barn, anxiously studying its pages in hopes to find some blissful solution of the dark, distressful questionings as to ' eternal things' which now harassed his spirit both night and day.

He had not been able to conceal his mental trouble from his parents ; but, pious as they were, they could not understand his melancholy mood, and fancied it boded ill for his sanity. So it befel one day that John Batty, a farm lad in Mr. Dawson's service, having passed through the barn and noticed William at his sorrowful studies, was anxiously questioned by the parents as to where he had seen their son, and how he was engaged ; and being informed, they proposed to remove the book from his keeping if they could. The two boys, different in position, were close allies in thought and feeling, so that John quickly apprised William of what had just passed.

' I was obliged to speak the truth,' he pleaded.

'You did right,' answered his friend; but he took care to find a hiding-place for *Doddridge* in the 'wall-plate' of the granary; and thither he now betook himself for his secret readings.   It was not very long before light began to dawn upon his spirit—a twilight glimmer at first, but still the true herald of the day.   He had made his life-choice— had 'solemnly surrendered himself to Almighty God,' and his voluntary offering was accepted, and his steps were guided into the path of peace.   A curious document, dated July 25, 1790, comprising a carefully written extract from Doddridge of the form for the 'Solemn Surrender,' and the appended words 'solemnly performed this day,' remained among William Dawson's papers, in proof of his endeavour to bind himself by lasting pledges, and put fences about his resolves to be God's liegeman, even at this very early period of his life.   He never did go back from the position thus assumed.

Dreams and visions helped him.   In his sleep he saw the Broad and the Narrow Ways lying outstretched before him; the first crowded with joyous throngs who danced along it in mirth and jollity, revelling in the fruits and flowers that enriched it; the second not only narrow and arduous, but almost deserted.   Many there were who urged the dreamer to enter the smooth, broad, pleasant path, but he refused; and seeing at his side his friend, John Batty, he said to him :

'We'll take the narrow path, John; it will do for us; ·
we shall be less incommoded in it.'   And in fancy he had already travelled some distance on it, with this congenial companion, when he awoke; and behold, it was a dream. But the dream had great power on his waking thoughts through many a year; and it was still vividly in his memory when, only a short time before his death, he met again the

boy-friend who had appeared in it. Batty had become a prosperous farmer, but prosperity had not diminished his religious earnestness and faithfulness; he was a zealous Class-leader, while Dawson was a widely popular preacher. 'Bless God, friend Batty, we are in the narrow way yet!' was Dawson's impulsive greeting of his boyhood's friend; and the allusion was well understood and cordially received.

A second friend now became very serviceable to Dawson; a young man named Samuel Settle, working for the corn-miller of Hillam Mill, was able to comfort the enquirer by telling him that it was possible to know one's sins forgiven, possible to be assured of the favour of God; for he himself lived in the enjoyment of such an assurance. To attain a similar blessing now became William Dawson's fixed desire, sometimes his half-despairing desire; but the time was not far remote when it should be granted.

'His convictions of sin were deep; . . . the foundation of his religion was laid in deep humility. . . . I shall never forget the marked attention he paid to the discourses from the pulpit,' is the testimony of his pastor of this period, the Rev. Thomas Dikes. This gentleman, on his removal to Hull, was succeeded in the curacy of Barwick-in-Elmet by the Rev. John Graham, of York, who in his turn became much interested in young Dawson, and helped him with counsel and friendship.

Happily for himself, the young man was keenly alive to the loveliness of the fair world, and often took pleasure in wandering about the fields. But, on one day of full summer splendour, his solitary stroll only made him more aware of the darkness of his conscience-stricken spirit. He was standing musing by the hedge-side in utter wretchedness, when his attention was drawn by the lively note of 'a little helpless, innocent bird,' no sweet singer, only some brown-

clad sparrow or wren, that hopped and chirped among the
bushes. 'Cheer up—cheer up—cheer up,' he fancied was
the burden of its humble song. 'The little bird is happy!'
ran his thoughts; 'and I—blessed so far beyond it—I, "with
higher thought endued"—I, an immortal spirit, born for
heaven—cared for by an Almighty Father—fed, sheltered,
protected, redeemed, with salvation within reach, and the
very heaven I was born for, offered—I am unhappy!' The
dark mood passed away, and a gentle, trustful peace of soul
replaced it. To him the little bird had been heaven's
messenger. Nor was it long before a fuller joy was granted.

He had, long ere this, ventured to approach the Table
of the Lord, though in much fear because of his un-
worthiness. Some time in the year 1791, he was again
kneeling before the Communion Table, while Mr. Graham
was officiating, and listened as that true pastor uttered the
comfortable words, 'The Body of our Lord Jesus Christ,
which was given for *thee*, preserve thy body and soul to
everlasting life, Take and eat this in remembrance that
Christ died for *thee*, and feed on Him in thy heart by faith
with thanksgiving!'

With these words a flood of light came into his soul.
How was it he had not long since appropriated the blessing,
here directly given to himself? He *saw* the love of God in
Christ Jesus, and it was enough ; the love of God entered
into his own soul by the Holy Ghost given to him. He was
born a new man in Christ.

It was well that this spiritual crisis passed so early. He
was not yet nineteen. In the same year the good Luke
Dawson was called away to his reward, and William found
himself called on to assume all his father's responsibilities.

He has left us a touching picture of his heart-sick suspense in those days of threatening bereavement, when it was

doubtful how the struggle for life would go, and he watched his mother's face, as she came out in the morning from his father's chamber, to see if it spoke hope or despair. 'Sometimes after a comfortable night there was a sunshine on the countenance ; sometimes after a restless night I could see a cloud and gloom upon it.' The *eldest of six*, William, had reason more than common for the anxiety with which he longed for a favourable issue ; the mother, sitting at the bed-head, might well sigh, 'Spare my husband !' the children might well wonder, with aching dread, who would now be their protector? who would provide for their needs? So it is that Dawson has depicted a family in circumstances like those he so vividly remembered, when 'the Rider on the Pale Horse had got his commission,' and must needs serve it even on the father and the husband. 'But there is one thing which may be said,' he adds, remembering the happier side of his own affliction. ' If He take the father, He will not leave the children fatherless ; if He take the father, He will not leave the widow without a husband. God is a Father of the fatherless, and a Judge to the widows.' The youth of eighteen was actually able to take up the work of the man of fifty. He succeeded to the stewardship of Sir Thomas Gascoigne's collieries, to the management of the farm connected with it, and to the headship of the bereaved family ; and though his younger brother could do something on the farm under William's supervision, the diary of the latter shows that he was constantly busy in the field as well as in the mine. Was it not well that he had attended to the 'Great Concern' before his leisure was invaded by the countless harassing details of this life's concerns, that furnish the crowded yet scanty records of his first months of manly responsibility ?

CHAPTER II.

THE spiritual guides to whom William Dawson was chiefly indebted during his boyhood were, as we have seen, clergymen of the Establishment; men whose ability, zeal, and high character strengthened the youth's natural love for the Church of his fathers. Its seemly rites and customs were, from long association, so dear to him that at this time the idea of an ordained minister preaching *without a gown* was odious to him. Yet he did not hold aloof from the informal gatherings preferred by his Wesleyan friends and neighbours; he often chose to listen to the untaught eloquence of a local preacher, and was often present at a prayer-meeting. Something of this freedom from prejudice may be traced to the fact that his own beloved pastor, Mr. Graham, had the good sense to work on lines like those of the Methodists. Not content with preaching both morning and afternoon of every Sunday, he gave masterly expositions of Scripture at night, to all who would come and hear him, in the schoolroom; and he held a 'select meeting'—half class meeting, half Bible reading—on the Thursday evening in a private house, encouraging and stimulating the members to speak, to expound, to engage in prayer. Here it was that William Dawson made his first essays at public speaking, and here he sometimes ventured to pray, using a printed form of prayer. In Mr. Graham's absence he sometimes conducted the meeting, and gave, in his turn, expositions of Scripture; after a time he began to write these out, and some specimens have been preserved. More imaginative and fervid than thoughtful, declamatory in style, and loosely constructed, they still are full of promise, and indicate what would be the excellences as well as the defects of his ripened eloquence.

From some of his Wesleyan friends he often heard the praises of that remarkable pulpit orator, the Rev. Samuel Bradburn, and his interest was sufficiently excited to make him take the opportunity that was afforded, at the Conference of 1793, of hearing Bradburn preach at Leeds, in the chapel where the Rev. E. Parsons usually officiated. The striking appearance of the majestic old man, his lofty stature set off by the flowing gown that he wore in compliance with the use and wont of the place, surprised Dawson into more admiration than he had expected to feel ; it was heightened greatly as he listened to Mr. Bradburn's discourse. Expatiating on the 'kingly office of Christ,' and on the harmonious order and working of the kingdom of God which He inaugurated, and over which He rules with resistless sway, the orator, by his skilful use of figures and illustrations drawn from the government of our own land, strongly enlisted the sympathy of the loyal and devout young Churchman, who also began to understand, from this example, how great is the power of direct, plain, heartfelt oratory, how great is the dignity of simplicity in speech.

Bradburn chose himself to give out two verses of the concluding hymn, setting aside the precentor ; and these verses, from an unfamiliar hymn of Dr. Watts, remained ever after impressed on William Dawson's memory—whether from the striking delivery of them by the preacher, or from the mingling of solemn triumph and childlike quaintness in the lines themselves—

'The government of earth and seas
    Upon His shoulders shall be laid;
His wide dominions shall increase,
    And honours to His name be paid.

'Jesus, the holy child, shall sit
    High on His father David's throne;
Shall crush His foes beneath His feet,
    And reign to ages yet unknown.'

Dawson came away from the chapel with a much nobler opinion of the Wesleyan itinerant ministry than he had previously entertained. In his rural seclusion he had probably formed his ideas of what a Methodist preacher might be from the excellent, but blunt and unlettered, class-leaders and local preachers he met around his own home. One of the former had much affronted him on a certain Sunday afternoon (when the preacher appointed failed to appear), by calling on him as 'Willy,' and bidding him 'go to prayer.' William Dawson promptly refused, with a feeling of anger that *he* should be asked to pray in a meeting unconnected with his own Church. His conscience, however, had pricked him, and reflection whispered that either pride or shame of an unbecoming sort had dictated the refusal. Not long after he had heard Mr. Bradburn, the same old class-leader again called on him at a prayer-meeting, pushing a hymn-book into his hand, and requiring him to 'give out a hymn, and go to prayer.' This time he complied, with diffidence and humility quite equal to his pride on the former occasion; but the ice was broken; and his career as a lay evangelist among *Methodists* was now really beginning.

The year 1795 saw him not only working hard in his vocations of colliery manager and farmer, but also sedulously cultivating his own mind; and it is interesting to see, in his list of book purchases, the productions of the Methodist press, both prose and verse, and notably the *Collection of Hymns for the use of the People called Methodists*, mingling with Doddridge's *Family Expositor*, Watts's *Hymns*, and the *Olney Hymns*. The noble hymns of the Wesleys, which so grandly embody a triumphant and living faith, the singular and pathetic grace of Cowper's sacred lyrics, the devotional tenderness and sweetness of good Isaac Watts, were a literary revelation to the young man hitherto acquainted only with the archaic quaintness and baldness of Sternhold and Hopkins, and with the more pretentious insufficiency of Tate and Brady, in their metrical versions of the Psalms. Admiration bred emulation; and Dawson began to try his own wings in short poetic flights, choosing always sacred subjects.

He judged these early attempts very harshly afterwards; but in the opinion of his biographer, Mr. Everett, who had access to them, they gave evidence of real though immature power, and were occasionally striking both in thought and expression, though the writer, lacking 'the accomplishment of verse,' had succeeded but indifferently with the poetic form he tried to give to his imaginings.

His studies were pursued not in the home at Barnbow, where too probably there was small chance of quiet seclusion, but in a sort of shed, since improved into a stable, which lay a mile away from the house, and which was suggestively called 'Grime Cabin'; for here the colliery accounts were kept and the colliery business transacted. The dusky hut served many purposes; it was William's office, his study, his oratory; and hither, every Sunday morning at seven, he betook himself, 'brushing with hasty foot the dew away,' to meet his faithful friend John Batty, that they might begin the holy day with praise and prayer, and take sweet counsel together. It was due to no divergence of faith that they did not afterwards walk to the house of God in company; but though John had already

3

cast in his lot wholly with the people called Methodists, William still clung to the parish church, where, in *the breaking of bread*, his Saviour had been made known to him ; there, then, he went to worship, while his friend betook himself to the humbler Wesleyan preaching-place at Garforth.

The lines of demarcation between Churchmen and Wesleyans had not yet been drawn so sharply and trenched so deeply as now ; it is clear, indeed, that at this time there was still clinging about the Anglican Church something of the spirit which had breathed its mightiest life into the Methodist movement—the vanishing day was not without a soft after-glow, for we find Dawson, the lay-exhorter, called on to take part in a very 'irregular' service, in which the glowing zeal of the Rev. R. Hemington, Vicar of Thorpe-Arch, expressed itself.   This pious man, honoured and loved through his forty-five years of ministry in that parish, was not content with the allotted routine of parochial duty ; he not only preached in the various churches, but would address congregations gathered together in barns and in private houses, and he did not disdain to call on William Dawson to engage in prayer, when his own sermon had been concluded, nor did Dawson, now well accustomed to pray 'without book,' hesitate to comply.   The little incident is a sufficient evidence of the position that the young farmer was rapidly assuming, as an able, sincere, and ready advocate of the Gospel.   He was probably not more than twenty-two years of age when he was thus distinguished.

Dawson's early friend, Samuel Settle, the youth from Hillam corn-mill, had, in 1795, definitely abandoned the business in which he had been engaged, and had been entered at Magdalen College, Cambridge, where he was now studying for the Church.   His letters to Dawson do not, in so many words, relate how he had been enabled to meet the necessary expenses, but many allusions make it certain that he was materially aided by what was known as the 'Elland Society,' the members of which, benevolent clergymen, made it their aim to bring forward pious young men of good intellectual promise but scanty means, and help them to the University career that should fit them for taking Orders. The headquarters of this Society were at the picturesquely-situated little town of Elland, near Halifax, hence its title.

Its character and operations are of some importance to us, for it was by means of this association that William Dawson's friend and pastor, Mr. Graham, was now planning to introduce his young fellow-worker into the Christian ministry. He had read and approved some of William's essays in composition, he recognised how great were his natural gifts as an orator, and he felt convinced that he was destined for higher work than that by which he was now earning his bread.

'I knew him intimately, and loved and valued him as a brother,' wrote Mr. Graham, when Dawson had passed away. 'His natural vigour and originality of mind, his clear and comprehensive views of Scripture doctrines and duties, his experimental knowledge of Christ and His salvation, and his solid yet fervent piety, seemed only to require a more regular and extended education to make him, what indeed he became without it, "a burning and a shining light."'

Having such an opinion of Dawson, Mr. Graham felt justified in suggesting to the young man that he should try to qualify himself for Orders.

'How would you like to change your drab coat for a black one?' he asked him playfully one day. William's answer made it clear that he would not shrink from such a change; so Mr. Graham went on to say 'he would recommend him to the "Elland Society," through the Rev. Miles Atkinson, of Leeds,' who was one of its members. The recommendation was duly given as far as Mr. Graham's power extended ; it was destined, however, to prove fruitless. The funds of the Society were low, and the length of time which elapsed while it remained altogether doubtful whether it could or would tender its assistance to Dawson daunted him, and ultimately led him to believe that *here* his divinely-appointed way was not to be found.

To one of his ardent and decided character it was no small trial to be kept, day after day and week after week, in complete suspense as to what his future career ought to be ; many entries in his diary witness how painfully he felt it. The 'strong inclination to enter the Church,' which he records soon after Mr. Graham had opened the subject with him, was combated by ever-recurring 'reasonings' as to the propriety of his seeking that 'longed-for employment.' The manner of Mr. Atkinson, who was cautious and prudent, and slow to commit himself by any pledges of support, chilled William's hopes just when they were beginning to glow. He had imparted his intentions to his mother, and evidently that excellent woman would interpose no hindrance, though her chief support would be withdrawn should he leave her for college. He had carefully enquired whether his brother would be allowed to fill his place at the colliery when he himself resigned it, and here too a favourable answer was returned ; but Mr. Atkinson's hesitating way of receiving his proposition hurt and repelled him. 'My pride rose,' says he in self-rebuke ; and then he records 'unbelief, fear, hope, and faith alternately rising in the soul ; sometimes thinking it the greatest folly to aspire after such an office, and at others cordially embracing. Jesus, guide me !

After all, praised be God, I can say, "Thy will be done."'

One incident that he sometimes related in after years, though it is scarcely indicated in the diary, must have had its share in inclining him to fall in with Mr. Graham's wishes, and to clothe himself with the recognised authority of the clerical office. He was in the habit, as we have seen, of conducting in Mr. Graham's absence the 'sort of cottage lecture' which that gentleman had set on foot in the school-room ; and here, as the pastor witnesses, 'his talents and gifts conspicuously displayed themselves.' Yet it was here that in the July of 1795 he met, from some person more officious than discreet, a sort of check, not very courteous, and only too intelligible.

On a certain Thursday evening Dawson had prepared and delivered a genuine *sermon* founded on a chosen passage of Scripture—Psalm lv., verse 6 : 'Oh that I had wings like a dove ! for then would I fly away, and be at rest.'

His own life, in its ceaseless round of irksome, anxious duties, its premature responsibilities, conjoined with the insight into others' woes which he had gained while piously ministering to the needs of sick and suffering neighbours, had well fitted him to understand the heartsick yearning embodied in those words of immortal pathos, which had often come into his mind while he watched the airy flight, or listened to the sobbing cooings, of the birds that fluttered around the dovecote at Barnbow ; and without doubt this first 'sermon' had that charm of intense feeling and vivid expression which may be found, by those who care to seek it, in every one of Dawson's published discourses. But some one must have listened in grim disapprobation. What right had this mere layman, this farmer without episcopal ordination, to take a text and preach from it like his betters?

Therefore, the next Thursday evening, Mr. Graham being again absent and Dawson to officiate as usual, the Bible was conspicuous by its absence. There should be no turning of its leaves and finding and giving forth of a text on this occasion! The layman might, if he chose, exhort, as the minister had sanctioned his doing; but there must be no more *preaching*!

The curious distinction, which was well understood in John Nelson's days, was understood as well in William Dawson's. He was deeply hurt, but refrained from expressing his wounded feelings for many a year; his diary even suggests that he rebuked himself for the pain he experienced.

'Spoke on Psalm lv. 6.—Well may a Christian wish to be at rest. In all I do, there seems to be something of pride mixed up with it,' is his only traceable comment on the annoyances of this day.

A difficulty for which he was by no means prepared met him when he essayed to begin the course of study proper for one who hoped to become a University man. Mr. Graham had advised him to get a Latin grammar, and try to master the language of old Rome; and William dutifully set to work on Ruddiman's *Rudiments*, devoting to painful study of its pages such leisure hours as he could find amid his multifarious occupations—the sowing and reaping, the leading and winnowing of corn, the making and stacking of hay, the buying, washing, and clipping of sheep, the business journeys to this fair and that, which his journals show, mingled with his punctually observed religious duties, and with the daily toil at the colliery, where it was his ceaseless anxious care to hold the balance level between the owner and the colliers, and to see to it that the latter neither did nor suffered wrong in any transaction. But the just and quick perception that served him well in these business matters, the manly intelligence that found lifelong delight in poring over Baxter and Bunyan, Alleine and Goodwin, Manton, and Butler, Wesley and Clarke, and many a noble Puritan and Evangelical divine besides, seemed wholly to desert him when he tried to master the mysteries of Latin declensions and conjugations and idioms. With something like despair, then, he went to tell Mr. Graham of his ill-success; 'he could make nothing of the Latin; he feared it would crack his brain.' The clergyman enccuraged him to persevere, notwithstanding this discouraging beginning; telling him truly that the first steps were always the most difficult, whatever the subject attempted; and, somewhat encouraged, Dawson struggled on as best he could, doubtless aided by advice and hints from the kind pastor, as well as from Settle at college, who wrote sympathisingly and hopefully, and helped the student to a Latin dictionary. Some progress was made, as a specimen of translation from the Latin in Dawson's diary for 1797 witnesses; but the study would probably be relinquished simultaneously with the student's hopes of entering the Church.

Indifferently as William Dawson succeeded in attaining the Latin scholarship held so essential for a clergyman, he was meanwhile quietly perfecting himself in qualifications at least as important for a shepherd of souls.

'Pure religion and undefiled before God and the Father is this, To visit the fatherless and widows in their affliction, and to keep himself unspotted from the world.'

His diary in its open simplicity of statement shows him tremblingly alive to the need of keeping his *raiment white* —alarmed at the first approach of sin, even in such insignificant commonplace forms as 'unsteadiness, peevishness, fretfulness, ingratitude,' and that *levity* which he deemed his *besetment*, though in another it would have passed unblamed by him as harmless gaiety, the overflowing of a cheerful nature. Meanwhile he was sedulously visiting William Smith, a needy dying saint, of whose long, useful, devoted career he afterwards wrote a short account; and when, after great and patient suffering, the humble Christian departed to be for ever with his Lord, William Dawson still continued his care for the poor bereaved wife, Hannah Smith, to whom, without acquainting his family, he managed three days in the week to convey his own dinner that she might enjoy a comfortable meal, while he, without her knowledge or consent, was fasting. This noble kind of self-denial was the more praiseworthy since Dawson, a stalwart, hardworking young man in the fulness of his strength, could not thus thwart his healthy appetite without real suffering. He did not offer to the Lord that which cost him nothing, when he thus, out of his own narrow means, ministered to the greater need of his sorrowing fellow-Christian.

When the year 1797 opened, Barwick was just being deprived of its excellent curate, Mr. Graham, who then obtained the preferment he merited. He was succeeded by a young Mr. Atkinson, who was zealous, liberal-minded, and useful, and who seems quickly to have singled out Dawson as a friend and fellow-worker. He lacked, however, the special gifts that had made Mr. Graham's friendship so precious to the devout young farmer; and the secret attraction which was drawing Dawson towards Methodism had the less to counteract it; while those hopes of entering the Church by the aid of the 'Elland Society,' with which Mr. Graham had first inspired him, did not long outlive that gentleman's departure. There was no door open that way. Letters from Settle, who was hard at work at Cambridge, spoke of the studies of the place with a kind of melancholy scorn, and were not calculated to lead Dawson to regret his own disappointment very deeply, or to make him covet the life at college from which he was shut out.

On the other hand, he came more and more under the spell of the great Methodist preachers of his day. Already, at Seacroft, he had heard Joseph Benson, who then and always produced on him an 'overwhelming effect.' There was a power in the sermon and in its preacher that was wholly new in Dawson's experience, and that dissolved him in tears despite his struggles to preserve a becoming composure. 'At length,' says he, 'I said to myself, "Let it come"—laid my head on the front of the gallery, and let the tears hail their way to the bottom of the chapel.' Now he heard this impressive preacher again, and others scarcely inferior to him—men such as Pawson, Mather, and Myles— and their discourses pleased and delighted him, so that he would steal off to catch some words from them after taking his part in his beloved Thursday evening meeting, which the new curate, Mr. Atkinson, had been wise enough to keep up.

But, accustomed all his life to the 'decency and order' of worship according to the beautiful forms of the English Church, Dawson felt some fastidious dislike in these early days for many of the modes in which Methodist fervour would show itself. He scarcely knew how to reconcile himself to the loud, frequent, irregular outbursts of stormy responses during praying or preaching, in which the strong feeling of those who heard found expression; and little did he anticipate the not very distant time when his own vehement oratory would produce effects as startling.

A zealous revivalist, W. E. Miller, came to Barwick and held a service; William Dawson went to that meeting in no unfriendly spirit, but he knew not what to think of the tumultuous character of the proceedings, or of what seemed their confusion. The rising tide of excitement did not bear him away with it ; he stood, sat, knelt a spectator only, and a critical one, watching everything that passed with con-centrated, keen attention. His attitude could not pass unobserved. Doubtless there was something rather formid-able about this silent, stalwart, sunburnt young farmer, whose dark full eyes shone coldly watchful under his massive overhanging brow, and whose firm mouth was closely com-pressed as he surveyed the agitated crowd before him without giving any sign of sympathy with their emotion.

Mr. Miller, while moving about at the close of the meet-ing among the kneeling groups, and addressing now one man, now another, noticed William Dawson with some appreciation and some displeasure. He had a blunt message for the powerful-looking but unsympathetic stranger, to whom he made his way, and, laying his hand on his head, said :

‘ Thou wilt do a great deal of good in the Church, when thy heart is emptied of pride.’

Dawson scarcely deserved the censure ; but the prophecy of his future usefulness showed some discernment on the part of the rough-spoken evangelist, whose words found fulfilment sooner than he probably expected.

That year the Wesleyan Conference was held in Leeds, and Dawson found means to attend the public services held in connection with it, when men such as Pawson, Bradburn, and Coke were the preachers. The fervour and power of their discourses drew him strongly, and quietly won his heart for the Church which produced such sacred orators. Ere long we find him attending a Sunday afternoon preach-ing at Barwick, in the open air ; then, being struck with the great possibilities of good in such services, he ventures on

out-door work himself; and, in conjunction with his boyhood's friend, John Batty, he begins to hold a series of
prayer-meetings in the neighbouring village of Scholes.

At one of these meetings appeared that simple-hearted,
fervent 'Village Blacksmith,' Samuel Hick, who called on
William Dawson to 'engage in prayer,' and was greatly
pleased with the young man's ready compliance, and with
the spirit of the prayer he uttered. Ignorant that this was
by no means the first time that Dawson had publicly joined
in a Methodist prayer-meeting, equally ignorant that to
Dawson was due the holding of these meetings at Scholes,
the good Samuel always took credit to himself for having,
on this occasion, 'brought out' the evangelist destined to
prove so useful, and on having fixed his sphere of work
among the Wesleyans.

No one tried to disturb the fixed conviction of his mind,
which gave him much innocent satisfaction, and for which
he could have adduced what looked like good evidence,
since within a very little time William Dawson was preaching
his first 'sermon' in public at Scholes, and to its Methodist
people. They had heard of his informal exhortations in that
schoolroom at Barwick, where to 'take a text' and *preach*
from it had been judged unfit for the laymen; but of that
nice rule the Methodists knew nothing, while they wished to
benefit by the vigorous addresses which it was said Dawson
could deliver. Being asked to preach to them he complied,
and delivered a sermon, which he had carefully written out,
on Prov. xxix. 25—'The fear of man bringeth a snare'—a
discourse which showed much knowledge of the foolish
human heart, and which closed with impassioned appeals, to
the young especially, not to be turned away from seeking
their eternal good through fear of the human comrades and
friends, who could render no help in the hour of death and

in the day of judgment, to the sinner misled by fear of human opinion into neglecting his own best interests.

A second sermon, composed about the same time, bears the stamp of greater power ; founded on Isaiah iii. 10, and referring plainly to the anger and alarm with which in that year, 1797-8, the proceedings of wild, revolutionary France were viewed by Englishmen, who saw themselves threatened with invasion, this discourse dwelt emphatically on spiritual perils darker and deeper than any which could endanger man's body or estate through the warring of nations, pointed to brighter rewards than any conqueror could win, and alike in warning and encouragement was pervaded by a fire which clearly foreshowed the coming orator.

These earliest ' sermons ' of Dawson were eagerly heard at Scholes and at Colton, and soon came requests that he would preach again, not only at these, but at many other outlying villages and hamlets. He did not turn away from the doors that opened to him, but gave his unpaid labours freely, whenever his toils as farmer and mining-agent permitted. Sometimes, as first at Colton, he spoke to a little company gathered in a friendly house, but soon the growing congregations which gathered to hear him made it needful that he should preach in the open air ; and he had his experience of the bold freedoms of open-air hearers. ' How do you know that ? ' was a question flung at him at Colton by a man standing on the outskirts of the crowd, as he spoke of the coming Judgment Day, and said sharp things of sinners ; and the unlooked-for interruption struck him dumb for a minute, till a friendlier voice loudly bade him ' Go on, go on,' and he recovered himself and his habitual courage.

Whitkirle, near Colton, was a frequent scene of his

hallowed toils, though before he visited it as a preacher, it was not included among preaching stations; and we find him at Swillington, at Preston, at Horton, at Garforth, at Aberford—sometimes speaking in barns and houses, sometimes from the door-step of a friend; crowding several services into the hours of one Sunday, and gathering with practice an energy and a power that showed themselves in a vehemence of delivery of which he was hardly conscious, and which he might not have approved in another.

His mother, the good Churchwoman, heard him preach, and complained afterwards of his 'shouting.' 'It quite distracts my head,' she said; 'I can do with anything but thy shouting.' Previously he had not suspected this in himself, and not long after he said to his mother, with some satisfaction, when his sermon was over:

'Mother, I have not shouted much to-night.'

'Shouted!' was her disconcerting answer. 'Why, child, I never heard thee shout so much before.'

And it became clear that the error, so wholly inadvertent, was not very likely to be soon cured.

CHAPTER III.

THE TIME OF DECISION.

NOW that he was in the full stream of work for the benefit of others, William Dawson found his own spiritual life brightening fast. He no longer underwent the torture of mistaking a resisted temptation for a committed sin ; he could remember now that even his sinless Master 'suffered, being tempted,' and in the fire of his active zeal whatever had been morbidly anxious in the character of his piety was burned away.

Something of this happy change might be traced to the fuller fellowship with like-minded Christians into which he was now entering, being drawn more and more into the inner life of Methodism. He had been won to make one in 'a little Christian fellowship' at Barwick, when it was led by a Leeds minister, Mr. Blayborne ; he attended love-feast after love-feast as the year went on, and, unrepelled by the 'irregularity' attending the services held by a female evangelist, he repeatedly listened, with great satisfaction and profit, to the popular and useful 'Miss Mary Barritt'* when she spoke in public at Whitkirle, Kippax, Sturton, and other neighbouring places.

Such new developments of his religious zeal were not wholly pleasing to his excellent mother. She had been willing to resign her claim on his filial assistance, when she could hope that her self-sacrifice would bring her the reward of seeing 'her Willy' numbered among the ordained

---

* Afterwards Mrs. Taft.

ministers of that Established Church which she loved with exclusive affection. That dream was passing away, and it could not console her for its vanishing to perceive how the son, on whom she had built such high hopes, was being insensibly drawn away from the Church and towards Methodism ; for she saw more clearly than he did the inevitable tendency of his growing taste for love-feast and prayer-meeting and out-door preaching. She could not, then, always forbear giving him 'a warm reception' when he came home from attending such irregular services ; but happily he could meet her displeasure with a quiet submissiveness that disarmed it.

He was not conscious of any heart-alienation from the Church of his childhood, for no such feeling, either then or afterwards, could find a lodgment in his breast ; and he was still over-conscious of some faults of taste into which his warm-hearted Methodist friends were now and then betrayed. His enjoyment of ' Miss Mary Barritt's ' discourse at Sturton was much impaired by the tumultuous after-meeting which followed the preaching ; and the eccentricities that marked the conduct of ' Sammy Hick,' excellent good man though he knew the *village blacksmith* to be, were a trouble to him at this period. He blamed himself, however, more than anyone else would have blamed him, when in conversation he said hard things of the ' noise ' at the prayer-meeting, or of the odd speeches in which Samuel Hick indulged himself at a Sunday afternoon service in Garforth. People took up his criticisms and repeated them, and he did not like them when they were thus echoed back to him, and resolved that he would speak no more in that vein.

And his sense of fitness was even at this time far more deeply offended by the occasional presence of an unworthy

clergyman as officiating minister in Barwick Church, than
by the loud enthusiasm of some simple prayer leader, or the
quaint rough sayings of some unlettered preacher, whose
integrity and sincerity were beyond question.   It was a pain
to hear an occasional sermon from the curate who had once
been his schoolmaster ; he knew the man too well.   'What
a sad state should I have been in under such a minister !'
he wrote, with grateful remembrance of those very different
pastors, Mr. Dikes and Mr. Graham, who had helped to
mould his Christian character.   Their influence on him
was still strong, but they were distant, and newer, nearer
influences began to be stronger ; while as he studied the
works of the saintly Fletcher he learned to understand
accurately what Methodist doctrine was, and from Benson's
Defence of the Methodists he gathered just ideas of the
discipline and the distinctive modes of worship among
Wesleyans.   He approved heartily what he read.

He lived now in a busy round of Christian duties.   In
the home he pressed on relatives and friends the matters
relating to their eternal peace ; in the daily intercourse of
man and man he lost no chance of speaking a word for his
Master ; he visited the sick and suffering among his fellow-
Churchmen with kindly zeal, and when death entered their
doors he was often invited, and never vainly, to pray and
speak in the house of mourning and on the funeral day, for
the comfort of the bereaved.

The imaginative power which gave him his peculiar
attraction as a preacher was now showing itself very plainly.
In a sermon preached about this time at Scholes, there
occurs a picture as vividly impressive as he ever drew of
the perilous state of the sinner, whom he likened to a man
blindfolded, walking on a bridge without battlements, and
in his blindness swerving from the straight path towards

the undefended verge, while 'crowds of diseases and acci-
dents are pressing upon him, and may, the next moment,
jostle him over into eternity'—and as his audience hung
spell-bound on the words that showed the sinner just
trembling on the very edge of the bridge overhanging a
raging torrent, the preacher cried out with startling energy :

'Lord, save ! or he perishes in the roaring, bottomless
ruin below ! '

Such strong word-painting is often more potent for
good on the mind of the average hearer than reasoning of
the clearest and the most cogent ; and here lay Dawson's
peculiar strength.

The active and successful evangelist could not escape
some molestation in his work ; and the existence of mali-
cious feeling against him now manifested itself in various
ugly ways.   Robbers entered his humble counting-house and
carried off the small sum of money in his cash-drawer ; a
calf belonging to him was wilfully shot dead ; a neighbouring gentleman, possessing much influence, forbade his
dependents to hear Dawson preach, on pain of dismissal,
and used injurious language to the preacher himself, who
had a hard fight against the temptation to retort with equal
bitterness, but was not much overcome by it, though apprehensive, through tenderness of conscience, lest perchance he
had 'sinned with his lips.'

This was not so great a trial, probably, as another which
befel him, when various frauds, the authors of which
remained unknown, were committed with reference to
property for which Dawson was partly answerable to his
employer.   His own unblemished character, proved through
long years of true service, was, however, his sufficient defence
against the suspicion of complicity in these frauds.

Sir Thomas Gascoigne, though he did justice to the

4

integrity of his agent, took displeasure against him for matters relating to his sense of duty towards God.

It was a time of great public uneasiness; the air was full of wars and rumours of wars ; Ireland was in a state of dangerous excitement; England was threatened with invasion from France. Dawson and his employer, like all good Englishmen, desired to do their part towards the national defence. Sir Thomas required that each of his tenants should find a man and horse for a troop of cavalry—a requirement met for the Dawson family by William's brother Richard, who himself entered the cavalry. In addition to this, the men employed at the colliery were to be enrolled as foot-soldiers ; and 'Mr. Porter, the head-steward,' appeared accordingly at Dawson's little office, and took down the names of all the colliers. One may fancy the scene—the excitement among the toil-begrimed workers, the busy importance of the man in higher office, the subdued agitation and earnest feeling of Dawson as he saw his humble associates chosen for work that might be as full of peril for the soul as for the body.

The newly-enlisted men were soon after summoned to Garforth, whither Dawson accompanied them ; and it would seem that he took occasion to speak earnestly and plainly for his Master to the forced recruits gathered together at Garforth, which, we must remember, was one of his regular preaching places. He could not in his true-hearted zeal let slip this chance of uttering a word in season to the men who *might* never hear such a word again. But news of his doings were carried to Sir Thomas, and that gentleman did not hide his displeasure.

William Dawson was troubled when the busy tongue of someone, who perhaps had reported *his* proceedings to his master, apprised him how unfavourably those proceedings were regarded. He rested, however, quietly conscious of his own right meaning. 'What I did,' he wrote, 'was, I believe, agreeable to the will of the Lord,' and he did not fear that injury would come to him in consequence of such obedience. Nor did it; whatever annoyance Sir Thomas felt and expressed, he knew very well the value of such a servant as he had in Dawson, whom he could not easily have replaced.

It is very characteristic that the matter thus referred to is dismissed with a few lines of Dawson's diary, while page after page is filled with records of searchings of heart as to the purity of his own conduct and motives. Sorely he dreaded becoming the slave of 'King Self,' and sacrificing the interests of others to his own.

He had been paid for some piece of good work; had he not been paid too highly? yet the price was such as he would gladly have given to another man.

Unwittingly he had let 'a bad shilling' pass through his hands. Had he been watchful enough?

He had smiled, when in a place of worship some odd expressions were uttered—he had spoken of some event as 'fortunate' rather than 'providential'—he had seemed asleep, when really awake, because the quiet rest of his bed was pleasant, and he did not wish to rise yet. Was not sin in all this? So tender, so quick of sense, was his conscience; yet there was little that was morbid in it.

The months rolled by, and brought the spring of 1798. And now came up, to be decided finally the question whether William Dawson should enter the Established Church as one of its ordained ministers, by the aid of the 'Elland Society.' It is very clear that Mr. Graham, and his successor Mr. Atkinson, were unwilling that such powers as William Dawson possessed should be lost to the Church which they loved. The influence of Settle, his intimate friend, rather tended in the other direction; for this excellent young man, having passed through his college course and attained the dignity of Orders, spoke of the path he had traversed as 'long and dreary, and without a flower to regale the senses,' and of its end as bringing 'poverty, contempt, and almost universal neglect'—melancholy words, which at a later and happier period of his career he must have retracted. At this time, however, they had their influence on Dawson.

'I have not told you,' wrote Settle, 'to go and get into the pulpit, and preach among the Methodists; but I have almost told you, to lay aside all thoughts of entering the Church. . . . You inform me, that you address a word now and then to the Methodists. Why is it only "now and then"? why is it not as often as possible? . . . You are ordered to Nineveh, but you seem resolved to go to Joppa. Apply this.'

There was nothing very ambiguous in such words.

Affectionately urged by Mr. Graham to visit him in York, William found time to repair thither on Saturday, July 27th, 1798. He filled the Sunday with devotional exercises, attending Church service twice, and hearing his beloved former pastor preach in the evening; but in the morning he had worshipped at the Methodist chapel, and this is quite significant as to the preference which was declaring itself in him. 'He had freer scope among the Wesleyans.'

Difficult indeed it would be to picture the vehement, impassioned William Dawson—loud of voice, energetic in gesture, picturesquely vigorous in his style of oratory—subdued to the level of decorous propriety that might befit a clergyman. He had tried to tutor himself and tame himself, he had striven for a well-bred calmness, whenever he took part in services conducted by the ministers of the Establishment ; but the restraint grew increasingly painful ; and more and more he leaned towards those very irregularities in worship which had once displeased him.

He returned from York, after conversing with Mr. Graham on his future plans, still much undecided ; but the day of decision was close at hand. On October 11th he received an intimation from his good pastor, the Barwick curate, that Mr. Atkinson the elder 'wanted to speak to him at Leeds about the Elland Society.' Five days later he found he could ride to Leeds and have this decisive interview. He was at the colliery that morning, and there too was his friend John Batty, waiting to receive a load of coal.

'John,' said William, 'this day is to decide whether I am to be a clergyman, or remain as I am ; ' and Batty, the fervent Methodist, at once proposed that they two should repair to 'Grime Cabin,' and pray together that William might be directed rightly in his choice. As they went, Dawson's inward thoughts found utterance. He began by saying how the best hours of the day, his best time for working, lay between eleven a.m. and two p.m.—if he lost this he lost the most valuable part of his day. And such a precious working-time he felt lay just before him—his young life was drawing near its noon, without having reached it— he was but twenty-five, and his powers were in their blossoming-time. 'If I should go to college,' he went on, 'I should be obliged to remain there three years—three years taken from the best part of my life ; and they would be a mere blank, as far as actual labour in God's Church is concerned.'

With this thought strong on his mind, Dawson joined his friend in seeking God in song and in prayer. The strong, sweet young voices joined in the hymn,

'Behold the servant of the Lord !
I wait Thy guiding eye to feel ; '

and in the spirit of that hymn they prayed. With a deep
sense of nearness to a guiding heavenly Friend, they came
forth, at last, from their dusky oratory ; and to John Batty's
great joy, William exclaimed :

' John, I believe I shall have to be a Methodist preacher
yet.'

Still impressed with this persuasion, the young evangelist
mounted his horse and rode off to meet Mr. Atkinson in
Leeds ; and what he learned in his interview with that gentleman only strengthened the impression.   The good clergyman
strongly wished to decide his young friend's wavering preference in favour of the Church, and he dwelt eloquently on
the superior claims of the Anglican Communion ; but he
could not show Dawson an open way to its ministry.   The
' Elland Society' was still too low in funds to render him
aid.   Here then was the alternative : to linger on through
years of uncertainty and comparative inactivity, working as
an occasional lay assistant to such pious clergymen as might
be willing to accept his help ; or to renounce the visionary
hope of becoming himself a clergyman, and by allying himself with the Wesleyans to find himself in full continual
work as a preacher of Christ.   As a layman, however
eloquent and popular he might be, he might enter no pulpit
belonging to the Establishment ; but every Methodist pulpit
would be open to him, whose soul was on fire with the
longing to plead with men for his Master, who felt that his
commission to preach came direct from heaven, and that he
would neglect it at his peril.

Musing on these things, Dawson rode homeward,
earnestly praying for heavenly direction.   The next day he
was summoned to an interview with his dear former pastor,

Mr. Graham, who was at Woodhouse visiting his sister-in-law, and who seems to have taken alarm at the news he heard about Dawson.   He requested a visit from him then, and earnestly pleaded against his uniting himself to the Wesleyan body.

'They were increasing the number of Dissenters from the Church of England, little as they might intend it ; and look at the disputes and dissensions among themselves ! '— for those were the days of Alexander Kilham—'how could any one of peace-loving, orderly spirit be at home among them ?'

The good clergyman grew warm and eager ; Dawson's own spirit took fire.   'I felt I had gone too far to recede,' he said in after years, 'and I employed a strong expression, which not only startled Mr. Graham's sister-in-law, but at which I afterwards trembled myself,' and little wonder.   'I will risk my damnation on it ! ' he exclaimed, referring to the lawfulness of his work among the Methodists, and to his intense conviction that he was only following the guiding hand of heaven.

Violent the expression was, and it must have sprung from violent agitation.   'Gave Mr. Graham a denial of entering the Church,' was all the record of this decisive conversation that Dawson entered in his journal.   But he felt the denial to be final, and he stood by it, notwithstanding the disapproval it aroused in many of his friends.   Mr. Settle was now in the neighbourhood, and William repeatedly heard him preach.   In their interviews it appeared that the friend whose own hints had helped to fix his mind was not quite satisfied, now the choice was made ; nor did he stand alone.   A little shaken, Mr. Dawson wrote for advice to the Rev. Joseph Benson, and received a kindly but curiously ambiguous answer, which left the matter 'entirely to God and myself,' said the enquirer. And now Mr. Dikes wrote, with no doubtful intention : 'Mr. Benson tells me the Methodists have more preachers than they want. Why should you be in such haste? . . . If your family do not require your attention, by all means accept the offer of the Elland Society—only, if you do accept it, you must comply with all their rules, and not preach among the Methodists.'

It would almost seem as if a new prospect of attaining Orders had opened since Dawson's interview with Mr. Atkinson. But whether this were so or not, his decision remained unchanged. He had been long in reaching it, but having reached it he stood firm. He would not renounce 'preaching among the Methodists.'

CHAPTER IV.

UNION WITH METHODISM.

THE close of the year 1798, which had been so memorable to Dawson, saw him reading for the first time the *Life of Wesley*, and distressing himself, something more than he needed, as to his own lack of the 'witness of pardon' which the great Evangelist held to be all-important for one who should preach the Gospel; for no one who has studied the simple records of Dawson's spiritual life can doubt that he had long been living by faith on the Son of God. Now, however, that faith was to be his in greater fulness. Not only the well-chosen devotional works which furnished all his reading helped him, but his intercourse with living Christians; not only the letters of Fletcher of Madeley, but the conversation of Mr. Thomas Stoner (father of the Rev. David Stoner), then resident in Barwick, led him on to see that he must not despise such light and hope as he had, but must press on to attain more.

He was soon to part acquaintance with that *Little Faith* which he himself has quaintly described, in its feeble, puny, purblind case, oppressed even by the small portion of light it could receive, as 'a little lad, sitting in the corner, with a bloodshot eye, and a green shade over it.'

'Preach faith till you have it,' said Peter Böhler to Wesley, 'and then, because you have it, you will preach it.' No one gave this counsel to Dawson; yet unconsciously he acted in its spirit, and found the same reward as Wesley.

Evidence is abundant as to his growing popularity

during the year 1799.   Seventy-five regular preaching
services stand recorded in his diary for that twelvemonth,
and forty written sermons, bearing the same date, remained
among his papers to witness how hard this busy yeoman
toiled with brain and pen to meet the increasing demand
for his public ministrations, which were rendered freely
in mere love to God and man, and were valued as much by
Churchmen as by Wesleyans.   The preacher's own position
was still undefined ; ' he fought for his own hand ' in his
Master's battle, being the accredited agent of no special
denomination.   This did not interfere with the general
admiration for his zeal and ability; but there were one or
two good men who disapproved of this hard-fighting free-
lance.

'He shall not preach in my house till he is united to the
Wesleyans'! pronounced Mr. Wade, of Sturton Grange ;
and in a fashion still more severe the old Methodist
preacher, Mr. Suter, expressed himself, when 'the friends
at Seacroft' asked him to announce at the morning service
that 'Mr. Dawson would preach in the evening.'

'Who is this Mr. Dawson ?   He is not regularly among
us ; we know nothing of him,' said the old man with some
acrimony.   Without doubt these things were reported to
Dawson.   A man of smaller soul might have been hurt and
disheartened, or might have taken lasting offence, especially
when he recalled how at Seacroft itself a congregation, disappointed of hearing the admirable Vicar of Thorpe-Arch,
Mr. Hemington, had gladly accepted William Dawson as
his substitute.   The only effect such rebuffs produced,
however, was to make their object anxious to define his
position clearly, and take away any stumbling-block which
good men found in his conduct.   So, slowly, hesitatingly,
yet certainly, he drew nearer to the communion in which he

could be most widely useful ; made himself acquainted with the class-meeting, attending it frequently ; and at last, in the summer of 1800, he joined himself to the Society. It was not, however, till eight months later that he was received, as an accredited local preacher, by Messrs. Pawson and Barber, then stationed in Leeds.

And it would seem that these gentlemen accepted him with an amount of caution, not to say coolness, which reflected something of his own long hesitation as to the decisive step. 'They gave me three appointments,' he said, 'and left it to myself whether to supply them or not.' Probably the knowledge of Dawson's lifelong attachment to the Establishment was the motive for this lukewarm reception of a very powerful and popular lay-preacher, whom his new patrons never dreamed of asking to deliver the usual 'trial-sermon.'

Mr. Pawson, it is noted, had had reason to speak very sharply of certain clergymen and their hostility to the name of 'Methodist'; the controversy had been public and recent, and its impression might well operate to William Dawson's disadvantage. He was not, however, either repelled or discouraged, but entered with a valiant heart on his new career, and found abundant success in it.

If we look a little more closely at his homely life during those years of hesitancy, we shall find it not devoid of picturesque variety. Sometimes in the coal-blackened garb of a miner he is seen descending the shaft of the colliery, to inspect the workings and see that all is safe and well ; and that duty over, he is hailed by one rough, hearty voice after another with the cry: 'Come, give us a word ! There are some of your children here, and they want a bit of bread !' and responsive to the call he stands up and breaks the Bread of Life to the hearers that cluster around—swarthy faces lit by gleaming eyes that sparkle out of the coal-black gloom, in the feeble glimmer of two or three tallow candles, which shine most strongly on the massive shape and head of the preacher, on his glittering eyes and glowing features eloquent with earnestness.

IN THE FEEBLE GLIMMER OF TWO OR THREE TALLOW CANDLES.—*p* 44.

Sometimes, in the different darkness of a stormy night, he is making his way towards a place where he should preach, and amid rain and wind and thunder loses himself on a great moor, and must trust to his good horse's better instinct to find the way. It is December, yet a sudden vivid flash of lightning strikes, or seems to strike, the head of his stout stick ; flash on flash follows, so rapidly that he   .

can see the face of the country and tell which way he must turn.

He comes to Barwick, where his waiting congregation is just at point to disperse. He addresses them straightway, telling them of the adventures of the road, and with prompt dexterity spiritualises the incident, so as to supply the lack of a sermon. Easy to guess how he could speak of one lost

'PUT IT IN . . . COVER IT UP!'—*p.* 46.

in the world's wilderness—lost, despairing, in peril—till what seems a chance yet more perilous proves his salvation, showing him the way of escape—some sudden stroke of bereavement, maybe, some alarming sickness, some unfavourable turn of fortune, and as by a lightning flash the lost wanderer sees his imminent spiritual danger, and sees, too, the way of escape. And without doubt such an ' improvement ' of the incident of the night would prove an efficient substitute for the sermon he had designed to preach.

Contrasting with such a scene we have some quaint ,
glimpses of the stiff opinions on 'minor morals' held by
some of our spiritual ancestors. William Dawson 'gloried
in the character of an English yeoman,' and was wont at
this time to dress as beseemed that character—in good sub-
stantial drab cloth, with top-boots, and on Sundays a ruffled
shirt. So habited, he was passing through a wood on his
way home from preaching, when he was met by an old man,
something of 'a character,' who laid a significant finger on
the ruffle adorning Dawson's breast, and bade him 'Put it
in, put it in, and cover it up ; it was a worldly adornment
that did not beseem one who was publishing the Gospel !'

An eye-witness in later days describes Dawson, 'the
Yorkshire farmer,' as entering the pulpit in a composite sort
of garb—orthodox clerical black and white neckcloth above,
yeomanly drab and top-boots below.   But even so he would
not have escaped all criticism.   John Batty recalled a walk
with him towards Garforth, where William was to preach,
and as they went along the field-path Batty saw with surprise
his friend unwind the neckcloth that propped his chin
according to the fashion of the day, take out the 'stiffener'
that kept it rigid and upright, and replace the limp neckcloth.

'What are you doing?' asked Batty.

'Nothing particular—only becoming weak to the weak,'
said Dawson drily. 'Mrs. W. sent me word I am not to
appear at Garforth again with a stiffener in my neckcloth.'

One may fear that the lady warred against the fashion
simply because it *was* the fashion, not from any sense of its
uncouth absurdity.   The little incident has its value in
showing how superior the fervent preacher was to those
vanities of dress, which to his fair critic seemed so very
important.   It reveals the man as truly manly, in 'bearing

with the infirmities of those who are weak,' instead of resenting them.

His unusual sensitiveness, even to the shadow of wrong, is seen in another matter befalling at his period. A neighbour had made, under Dawson's auspices as Sir Thomas's agent, what seemed not unlikely to prove a hard bargain for himself about the taking of a limekiln. True, the man had been fully and fairly warned, and entered into the engagement of free will; but that even so he should perhaps suffer wrong in the matter was intolerable to Dawson, through whom the business was conducted.

There were other troubles during those few decisive years; troubles with the farm, when, through the unfavourable weather, the wheat sprouted in the sheaf; troubles in the home, when the brother who had undertaken to meet the family responsibility, in providing a 'man and horse' to serve in the 'Barleston Ash Volunteers' for the country's defence, withdrew himself from that corps, and brought his kinsfolk in danger of their employer's displeasure. Richard Dawson had good reasons for his withdrawal; but the step was felt distressfully by his hardworking elder brother and his mother. But outward annoyances like these passed over and were gone; no lasting harm came to the faithful household and its self-denying head.

Stories were afloat, too, that William Dawson's mind was turning towards marriage, and doubtless his 'young man's fancy' had its wistful, wandering dreams of wedded love and a wedded home, in these years of his prime.

He had no touch of self-torturing asceticism in his mood, to make him deem that earthly bliss was essentially and of necessity a sin. But 'that which he considered perfectly lawful in itself, he concluded to be imprudent in him, because of his temporal affairs, and more especially the position in which he stood in reference to his mother, and the younger branches of the family.'

For such reasons he put stern restraint on every errant imagination, and would bring no young bride to the house, where he could just maintain his excellent mother in rightful comfort. Mrs. Dawson's life was prolonged till William's habits had become fixed ; and when she passed away, he still had to think of a brother, Thomas, too much his inferior in energy of mind and character to dispense with his fostering care ; while his own abundant labours as an evangelist, which had brought him wide popularity, had brought him no money advantage, rather the reverse ; and he resolved to contract no such new responsibilities as he might prove unable to meet. So he lived and died, the head of the family, with all the cares of headship, but with comparatively few of its joys ; and he counted that prosperity to be well lost which might have been his, had he thrown into some well-paid business the zeal and energy with which he had proclaimed the Gospel of Christ.

His many published letters include not a few addressed to women, both young and old ; they are written with the transparent sincerity of a spiritual father, anxious only for the well-being of an interesting child 'in the Lord,' but there is a chivalrous tone about them which suggests what his courteous manner to his female friends might be, and one can understand easily how he became the subject of not unfrequent banter as to his supposed matrimonial designs. In such word-play, however, he could give as well as take, and the jester who attacked him had not always the best of it.

'What, I am told you have been disappointed in a love affair !' said an elderly friend, himself unmarried.

'That, according to report, is only *one*,' answered

Dawson with a quick, sparkling glance; 'but I am informed your disappointments have reached the *teens*!' and there was enough of truth in the retort to make it bite, and turn the friend's joke against himself. Let us hope he could laugh at it with a good grace.

The year 1800 had opened somewhat sadly for the Dawson household, several of its members suffering from a fever, which touched William himself twice; but the ensuing months seemed to brighten as they passed. The number of places that Dawson visited as a preacher increased rapidly. Sturton, where Mr. Wade had stiffly objected to him, now gladly received him; and his recognised and accredited position as a member of Society and a local preacher brought him new duties, new interests, new associations, full of quickening power, which well replaced the grace, orderliness, and picturesqueness that he loved in the services of the Establishment from which he was being insensibly weaned.

It was on July 18th, 1800, that William Dawson first appeared as a preacher in Leeds, in 'the old chapel,' and during the ensuing Conference there befel him an undesired experience which showed the rapid increase of his popularity. At Tadcaster he was called on to take a service in the stead of a 'travelling preacher' who had been announced, but did not appear in time. No sooner was Dawson fairly committed to the service than he saw two itinerant ministers, faultless in clerical garb, enter discreetly and take their place as hearers. They had delayed their entrance designedly, intending to hear the lay-preacher rather than to officiate themselves. Dawson was naturally disturbed by this, but his embarrassment was soon banished by the thought of the message he had to deliver; and the unwelcome hearers enjoyed as they had designed the full tide of his ready eloquence.

5

It was at this Conference that Dawson heard Bradburn preach 'for the last time' in Mr. Parsons's chapel. Bradburn, whose occasional eccentricity was at least as remarkable as that ascribed, not quite justly, to the 'Yorkshire farmer,' showed it unpleasantly on this occasion, when he chose to rid himself of the encumbering clerical gown in which he had preached so as to destroy it before the dispersing congregation—'doubling his elbows by his side, clenching his hands before his breast, having taken a portion of the gown in each, suddenly sending forwards his elbows and shooting out his back, so as to rend the gown from the shoulders downward'—the garment fell in ruins about him, and with it fell every wish on the part of the spectators to listen again to the admirable preacher whose humorous impulse had so overmastered his sense of what was due to the feelings of others. The grotesque spectacle would not be lost on Dawson ; himself humorous and impulsive, no such mistake is recorded of him. An innate sense of propriety always kept him from buffoonery, and however homely might be the illustrations he chose to use, they were made to convey an impression of awe. 'It was a solemn responsibility to listen to such sermons,' said a frequent hearer when questioned as to the effect of his preaching ; 'its intense earnestness was so unmistakable.'

It was a rough every-day simile which he used to reprove the sin of drunkenness ; but how powerful !

'Suppose yourself to be a servant, and your master were to come in the morning and bid you make a strong chain ; on the following morning he came again, and urged you to get on with it, and then day by day you were ordered to do the same job.

'Suppose that while you were working a person came and asked you if you knew what the chain was for, and you answered, " No ; as long as you got your wages you did not care " ! " But," says he, "it is your master's intention to bind you with this chain in everlasting bondage "—would you add another link to it ? '

' No !' said the drunkard thus addressed, 'all the money in the world would not hire me to do it.'

' Well then,' resumed Dawson, 'drunkenness is the devil's chain with which he binds sinners in perpetual bondage ; and whether you know it or not, every drunken frolic is a link added to the chain, and Satan will wrap it round you red-hot !' a suggestion which startled the hearer, and which did not pass away with the moment.

' I am adding another link to the chain !' was the thought that troubled him when he had been tempted to another and yet another ' cheerful glass ' too much. At last it became unbearable, and he broke the 'devil's chain'— not too late. The convert published the facts himself, call-ing his story ' The Tale of a Reformed Drunkard.'

The same simile was employed with terrific effect in the pulpit, in reference to the whole course of an erring life ; the sinner, despite every warning, taking pleasure in forging the chain for his own bondage, which, at the Day of Judgment, white-hot from hellish flame, should be drawn forth and coiled ' round, and round, and *round*' the writhing victim, who, by its weight, should sink 'under the surface of the burning lake for ever !' No thought of the ludicrous was suggested as the preacher heightened his voice till it rang like a trumpet peal with every turn of the chain ; his intense earnestness, his impassioned conviction redeemed his utter-ance from any suspicion of vulgar exaggeration. His simplicity of language and graphic force are apparent in all the few printed discourses from his pen now accessible ; the testimony of eye and ear witnesses helps us to judge how

much his solemn and impressive though dramatic delivery
added to the power of those plain-spoken addresses.

He now came under the immediate influence of the
saintly Bramwell, who was appointed to the Leeds Circuit at
the Conference just mentioned.   Dawson so admired Mr.
Bramwell's style that it greatly influenced his own.   ' I
thought the fire of his genius never blazed so brightly as
when he was addressing *The Sinner*,' he says, and speaks
of Bramwell's ' natural talent for poetry,' and his speaking
' in a sort of blank verse for twenty or thirty lines together,'
when denouncing the wrath of God on the children of
disobedience in strains of appalling grandeur.   These utterances impressed Dawson more deeply than the softer,
sweeter tones of invitation with which they alternated ; yet
both found their reflection in his own favourite efforts.

His growing acceptability as a preacher made him think
seriously that it would be his duty to devote his whole
energy to the one great work for which he was fitted in
every way, and this feeling is mirrored in his diary.   It is
at this time chiefly a record of anxious heart-searchings.
' That frame when I feel nothing but my *want of feeling*,'
' shame for my unprofitableness,' ' my want of real vital
godliness,' ' overcome with a fit of *lightness* ' (one may
venture to read instead : gaiety of spirit, natural to the
man) — such entries follow one another with touching
frequency.   But amid them we find how on a bitter
March day, when there fell a great snow, Dawson, unable
to pursue his usual toils, ' opened his mind to his family in
some measure ' — with earnest prayer to be guided aright
in the choice he was making,—on the subject that now filled
his thoughts.

It could be welcome to no one in the home circle : not
to the aged mother, the decorous Churchwoman, who had

been willing to surrender her best helper to the *Church*, but could not so heartily approve his irregular ministrations ; not to the helpless brother Thomas, who all his life long had to lean on William, the stalwart head of the family ; not to the younger lads and lasses. One can fancy the serious, almost sad faces, that turned wist ul eyes on William Dawson as he hesitated and half expressed the design so serious in its import for them, while the great snow, fleeing and whirling outside the window, shed its pale gleam into the room. Little, perhaps, was objected at the moment, but at night, perhaps, something was risked in the way of querulous remonstrance that wakened 'a start of angry grief' that made him groan ; and day after day there are hints of a temper not unallied to this on both sides, carefully veiled, but significant. He was more troubled about his own failures in slight matters of duty than about any deficiency of others.

'Blamed myself for allowing a slight spirit of murmuring to arise in my breast,' 'for not going to J. Barmiston's funeral' (where some profitable word *might* have been spoken), 'a friend came over, from whom I received no good,' 'should have warned him *more* solemnly' (*some* admonition clearly was given).

It was an exquisitely sensitive conscience that lodged in the broad breast of the good yeoman, but not a morbidly sensitive one ; he was not always writing bitter things against himself by any means, and it was when he was engaged in preaching to the little scattered congregations of the country villages around his home that he found 'a sense of nearness to God '—while he was in secret prayer it was that 'comfortable verses' would suggest themselves to his fancy— while he was busy with devotional readings that he felt enabled to 'surrender his all to God.'

It is with interest we note that Wesley's *Christian Library* supplied him with such works as those of Dr. Goodwin, which delighted him extremely; that very catholic collection of devotional and narrative reading was in its day of not a little service to men such as William Dawson, of more intelligence than means, and thus well answered Wesley's aim in publishing the collection.

The year 1802 opened on him in the full tide of his various occupations; there was no *melancholy void* in his outer life, and the inner world was exquisitely alive. The 'piety, talent, and zeal,' which only became more apparent as time went on, were such as fully justified the action of the Rev. M. Barber, when at the March Quarterly Meeting in Leeds he proposed William Dawson 'for the itinerant work.' The candidate, already so well-known as a voluntary itinerant, was unanimously accepted.

More attention was inevitably drawn to him, and his ministrations now took a much wider range, while the large chapels in Leeds, then thronged with eager hearers, often claimed his services. He did not, therefore, intermit his home duties ; at farm, at market, at colliery, he was still the busy, competent, incorruptibly honest worker ; he was the same faithful visitor of the sick, the same cheerful lightener of gloomy hours for the poor downfallen inmates of the workhouse, the same in steady attendance at the classes ; and, in this a true *Wesleyan* Methodist, he was if anything more sedulous in the recognised duty of fasting at stated intervals. Studying the *Directions to a Candidate for the Ministry*, which breathes the austerely Puritan spirit uttered through Cotton Mather, he tried conscientiously to shape his course thereby; and, more anxious than usual to order his life so as to avoid all that was unfitting a candidate for so high an office, he was not unnaturally more anxious, and more oppressed with doubt and dread, as to his own religious character than ever.

'Let me *die*, Lord, rather than live to grieve Thee, or bring the slightest stain upon my soul!' 'Afraid lest I should prove a castaway after all.' 'Nearly in despair'— such entries alternate with those that tell of his longing to see a chapel erected at Barwick—where, as so often in villages, it was hard to meet with a suitable piece of ground— and with the continual questionings of his mind 'how far it is the will of God that I should be a travelling preacher.'

Very touching is his prayer for direction, that the darkness of his understanding might be overruled and his way made *plain* before him ; he sought instruction and blessing through prayer and fasting; and what he sought was granted, although it was not wholly what he desired.

The extreme distress of mind which agitated him at this time was a little soothed when studying Bunyan's *Grace Abounding*; he found his own experience mirrored in that of an illustrious servant of God. But for the light given by Dawson's *Journal* it would be hard to believe that he, so well-remembered as the picture of bodily and spiritual health, racy in speech and keen of wit, had been able to sympathise with sufferings like those of the great dreamer, and indeed he was never so nearly mastered by maddening suggestions of impossible sin as was Bunyan. It is a touch of vivid Bunyan-like feeling, however, which breaks out thus :—' God raise me up ! I would not sin against Thee. My heart seems to say—though I may not wish what is said—I would rather be in hell without sin, than be in heaven with it.' The outburst was dictated by broodings over a past life which to the outward view was more than blameless, while in the present the mourner was zealous in all good works. Amid all the agitations of his mind,

Dawson succeeded in 'dismissing all his reasonings and committing the whole case to the Lord,' while the year ran on to the day of decision.

The dear mother, seeing her son very busy in securing a site for a 'preaching house' at Barwick, where 'Mr. Beanland's barn' was the best substitute, and the erection of a chapel in its stead was planned, felt a cheerful confidence that 'Willy' would not leave her yet, but must stay to superintend this scheme. He noticed the light of hope that shone in her looks, and was saddened; for now he was giving 'a cool consent' to beccme an itinerant, and now seeking Sir Thomas Gascoigne 'to obtain his acceptance of my brother Thomas in my place as steward of the colliery.' Everything seemed settled; he was accepted as a candidate by Conference, which met this year at Bristol, and it was indicated that his first appointment would be to Wetherby, near Leeds.

And yet all was overturned. Going to Sir Thomas's head-steward to close his accounts, Dawson found that the verbal prcmise to bestow his situation on his brother Richard, and so to ensure the comfort of his family, was not going to be kept. 'Oh, we can do without your brother's services,' said the steward coldly. Instantly it flashed into Dawson's mind that here was some underhand scheme which he would counteract. His dark eyes shot lightning.

'Well, then, I'll remain!' said he, 'and you may give me lower wages if you think proper!'

The steward looked, and was, confounded. He had meant to bestow the vacant situation on a relative of his own. Now it was not vacant.

Dawson left the office with the unalterable determination to stand by his own people. To forsake his mother and her children, *that* never could be the will of God, since his departure would mean poverty for them. He wrote promptly to Mr. Barber, apprising him of every circumstance, and announcing that duty to others bade him renounce his long-cherished hope of itinerating ; and he remained henceforth, as he quaintly but quite truly said, 'a Travelling Local Preacher.'

It is quite possible that Sir Thomas never knew all the circumstances that led his under-steward to retain the post he had been wishful to resign. For some reason, however, that gentleman now added thirty acres of serviceable grass-land to the farm held in connection with the colliery, assuring Dawson at the same time that 'he should have the additional land at a rent that would not hurt him,' a promise kept in the letter; if not quite in the spirit, it was probably not wholly Sir Thomas's fault.

Not a year afterward, we find Dawson 'at Aberford the whole of the day, waiting to take the farm at the advanced rent,' a farm sufficiently high-rented before, with the exception of the grass-land aforesaid ; and the next item of business is that the colliery would be 'set down,' in consequence of one of the strikes for wages that have been named, and the under-steward's services for a time in abeyance. Dawson might have said, 'All these things are against me!' but was content to pray, 'Lord, undertake for me and mine !' and his prayer of faith was not in vain. Yet another trouble was to befall him. Going to Kippax to preach, 'the mare fell *under* him, and *upon* him,' crushing the rider's leg severely.

'Bless the Lord, for His hand of love that was over me for good !' wrote the sufferer, knowing that matters might have been much worse. Undaunted, he went on to Little Preston, his next appointment ; but the injured knee resented such usage by swelling so much as to disable him for a time

from all exertion.   No murmur escaped him.   And in the
same gallant spirit he met the threatenings of adversity ;
sturdy industry, strict economy, and quiet trust helped him
to conquer,   He was never allowed really to suffer for the
devotion to homely duty, which had made him renounce his
most cherished desires.

CHAPTER V.

A MID the pressure of personal cares, Dawson never lost sight of the interests of the cause he loved ; it would actually seem that these occupied a far larger space in his thoughts than his own concerns. The chapel at Barwick, the purchase of a proper site for it, the entire management of its erection, the collection of moneys for it, the ceremonies of its opening in 1804 by ' Mr. Taylor '—these were the things on which he gladly expended his strength and his energy, and which filled him with joy when they prospered under his direction, as the entries in his diary witness. Without his presence and his tireless help the enterprise had never been carried through ; and here was apparent another reason why it was well that he had resolved 'to dwell among his own people.' His beautifully-kept collecting-book, with its headings of Scripture passages, enforcing the great duty of Giving, on every page, showed with what energy and industry, and in what lofty spirit of piety, he had toiled at the trying work of gathering, in tiny sums often, the many subscriptions which made up a large total by the April of 1805. The foundations of that modest ' preaching-house ' were laid in prayer and its gates set up in praise ; exulting in his success in *this* work, Dawson neglected to chronicle some matters that sharply touched himself ; but he noticed with much distress the threatened severance of the saintly Bramwell from the Methodist communion, that holy man being alarmed at the supposed invasion of the Church he loved by 'worldliness,' and being with some difficulty persuaded that his fears were groundless.

With such entries, evidencing his intense pre-occupation with the matters of the Kingdom, Dawson's *religious* diary closes, and now we must consider the man as others saw him—not the anxious watcher over his own heart, but the impassioned, fervent preacher, whose dramatic, imaginative oratory secured for him every year a wider circle of admirers. His 'parish' soon comprised a large section of the West Riding, and the crowds that gathered to hear him were often so large that no chapel would hold them, and he must preach in the open air.   Let us listen in fancy to one of these attractive discourses.

We are in the front rank of the throng, glad so to get standing room.   Behind us is a man who leans on a short staff, and listens with glistening eyes and chuckling murmurs of applause.   Dawson, preaching from 'Thou art weighed in the balances and found wanting,' is trying one class of sinners after another by the test of 'justice, mercy, and truth.'   Formalist, hypocrite, open flagrant sinner—all are tried in his nicely-poised scales, all are set aside as 'wanting,' and our neighbour chuckles gleefully, 'Light weight! short again !'   But now the preacher speaks of those who make loud professions of piety, but shame their profession by using 'false weights and false measures.'   Ah! what ails our neighbour?   He is mute ; his face works strangely ! He is a travelling pedlar, and that well-worn staff of his is made to do duty as his yard wand still, though it is long since it measured a good yard ; yet his show of zeal for religion is great, and Dawson is his favourite preacher.   His agitation is noted at once by the quick, glittering eye of the orator ; Dawson remembers his face—often has he seen it—remembers how the man has earned his nickname of

'Short Measure,' but not therefore will he shrink from con-
tinuing his discourse as he had designed. He presses on
the description of such a sordid sinner—he places him in
the scales, weighs him, finds him wanting! There is a

HE TOOK HIS CHEATING YARD-STICK, AND SNAPPED IT ACROSS HIS KNEE.
—*p.* 61.

sharp crash, a cry—the pedlar has taken his cheating yard-
stick, has snapped it across his knee, has flung the fragments
from him, saying, 'Thou shalt do so no more!' eloquent
testimony to the power of conscience, and to the very practical power of Dawson's words.

Some would rather dwell on such a result than on the fainting and the terror produced by the famous sermon, "Death on the Pale Horse," when the description of the grim rider steadily tracking his victim along the Broad Road had hushed the hearers into such silence that the ticking of the clock was clearly heard, and the preacher, catching the sound, cried, 'Hark! there is his untiring footstep!' and pictured how those rapid hoof-beatings gained on the sinner, overtook him, the fatal blow was struck, and there was the dying shriek, 'Lost! lost! lost! Time lost! Sabbaths lost! means lost! soul lost! Heaven lost! *All lost*—and lost for ever!' It was terrible excitement that was produced by this appalling climax, and the preacher had some difficulty in tranquillising those whom his pictorial eloquence had startled into a sense of their imminent danger. But we may not dare to tax the orator with 'sensationalism.' From his own deep conviction he spoke, and the danger he depicted was too real ; it was well that for once he made it manifest, and those who had thus been awakened did not relapse into their fatal indifference again. Very many were the 'spiritual children' of this fervid evangelist.

There is a strong tradition of a far different effect produced by him in a dramatic presentation of the story of David and Goliath, when he chanced to be preaching among the woollen-weavers of Pudsey village, near Leeds. These homespun folk were hanging entranced on his lips ; for, personating the boy-champion of Israel, he had struck down the vaunting Philistine, in whom he bade them see the type of all who exalt themselves against God ; and stepping back, and looking down as on a prostrate foe, he poured eloquent reproach and scorn on the fallen enemy of God and good, heaping taunt upon taunt, while the hearers waited breathless for the final fatal blow that he seemed preparing.

'Off with his head, Billy!' shouted a rough voice. Its owner, thirsting for the enemy's blood, would bear suspense no longer.

The sudden cry startled Mr. Dawson, and he had some trouble in going on after this quaint testimony to his powers; otherwise, it is said, the interruption might have passed unnoticed, so rapt were the hearers. But the ludicrous incident made the preacher shun that pulpit in the future. 'Levity,' he greatly feared, might overpower him should he revive such an association.

With the vivid picturings of the doom of an unrepentant sinner, in which he excelled, there alternated the most exquisite descriptions of the unwearied compassion of the Saviour. Nothing could be more touching than an exposition Dawson once gave of the lovely words, 'He shall feed His flock like a shepherd,' when, drawing on his own experience, he made his hearers see the starlit frozen fields over which moved the dark, shadowy form of an anxious seeker, the shepherd, wandering in search of what at last he finds—a poor, benumbed, perishing lamb, voiceless and helpless, till, gathered into the shepherd's arms, warmed and cherished in his breast, it can faintly bleat; type of the perishing soul, gone astray in the wilderness world, but sought, and found, and gathered into the Good Shepherd's breast, by His Spirit's power; and then, then only, able to utter the faint, bleating cry, 'Mercy! mercy! mercy!' a petition how quickly heard—how surely granted!

By such mingling of tenderness with terror, the preacher appealed to hearers of varied temperament—to the timid and apprehensive, to the stolid and the sturdy—these needing encouragement, as those required awakening. His published discourses show us, what we might not so readily gather from other sources, that the very sermons best remembered for their awe-inspiring character would end in sweet or glowing descriptions of the joy and peace promised to the penitent believer; while others, beginning with the joyful proclamation of ' Full and Free Salvation,' would terminate with denunciations of the grievous sin incurred by rejecting that pardon, and of the heavy consequences such sin must entail. There is something even now in his words, coldly as they stand on the printed page, which can awaken both hope and fear, and can strongly agitate the reader ; so that we may measure in some small degree what their spoken power would be ; and we do not wonder that it is said :

'His ministry was not so much remarkable for awakening a general excitement, as for producing individual conviction,' an infinitely more valuable thing ; for we see that his appeal was always to the individual conscience, and was eminently practical.

Hear him setting forth the evil of 'sowing to the flesh.' He bids us look at a madman who, in his plot of good ground, industriously sows nettles, thistles, all noxious weeds ; week in and week out he is at the work. Is not that folly enough? But there is something more. When the wicked weed-growth has come to its full and monstrous growth, it is to be gathered and heaped into a pile, in the midst of which the unhappy sower is to be burned to ashes. Is he not something more than mad thus to prepare his own doom ? ' Never was such a madman in the world !' says the hearer. Behold your own conduct! retorts the preacher. *You* are sowing to the flesh ; such a harvest *you* shall reap. If you persist in sowing sin what can come of it but destruction? The madman's fate will be yours. The seed you are now sowing will furnish fuel to consume you at last !

Passionately he pleads, 'Awake to see the evil nature and the dreadful end of a life of sin!' and then, with his magical change to the most winning persuasion, he tells of that *sowing to the Spirit* from which we may reap Eternal Life : dwells on the bliss, the glory of the Harvest-home of heaven. What is sowing to the Spirit? It is Well-Doing, in which you are not to be weary; 'in due season—just when the harvest is ripe, just when it is the proper time—you shall reap. And what will be the harvest? Life Everlasting!' and in colours so softly bright does he paint the harvest-joy of the redeemed, the gladness that is theirs in the presence of the Lord of the Harvest, that indeed the whole passage might be used in reproof of those who would rank 'Billy' Dawson with the coarser kind of untaught pulpit orators.

Once more let us listen to him—he is uttering his 'Warning to Youth.' Nothing more blunt, plain, fearlessly outspoken than his description of the perils that may assail young men and maidens if they do not keep clear of those 'whose mouth speaketh vanity, and their right hand is a right hand of falsehood,' of the irretrievable betrayals that may follow on small guilty compliances—of the sophistries by which people cheat themselves into ruin. Penetrating and stinging, the discourse is like a rough sea-breeze dispelling unwholesome vapours. We read without surprise how men brought their 'cases of conscience' to be decided by this preacher, and got clear, plain counsel from him. Such an incident is quoted in this sermon, of a young man much distressed because, long since, he defrauded his employer of £13; he had never been detected, now he earnestly wished to repay with compound interest, but how to do it rightly, the master being since insolvent, and his affairs in the hands of assignees? Dawson's reply was quick

6

and clear: 'Your master was no insolvent when you robbed him; your business is with *him*.' But in this very 'Warning,' directed against sordid, commonplace evils too commonly ignored, we find an exquisitely felt tribute to the beauty of Christian womanhood, to the hallowed power that the true mother-love of a Christ-like woman can exercise. His picture of ugly sin in its deformity would have lacked some of its power, if he did not oppose to it this other portrait of lovely virtue; and his homely language takes on a poetic charm as he dwells on the beloved ideal, in a manner that must have been very winning, and that evidences true refinement of feeling.

It was no vulgar humorist who left us such discourses; no mere sensationalist who understood so well that it was not enough to alarm because of threatening danger, but that you must point also to fair excellence that might be attained, if you wished to produce a lasting effect on the individual—hope being a nobler, stronger motive than despair.

But excellent as Dawson's methods might be, he refused to boast of their success. What if numbers had received a sense of sin forgiven under his ministry? The praise surely was not all his; 'he had reaped,' so he would have said, 'where others had sown,' and sowing had been vain, reaping impossible, but for the Divine Spirit, working invisibly who could say how long? So he would not number up his converts and proclaim their sum—it was too like David numbering the people; and he could utter sharp reproof when successful 'revivalists' seemed to arrogate any glory to themselves. 'Never boast of "souls being born under you," that were prepared by others! you only entered upon other men's labours; they would have remained unborn for you,' he said sternly to such boasters on one occasion. This 'popular' preacher would not suffer any depreciation of the quiet workers who won little praise.

Such as we have tried to paint him—not only eloquent, fervent, self-devoted, but self-forgetful and lowly-hearted— Dawson was an advocate whose adhesion must greatly benefit any cause ; and well was it when in 1813 his enthusiastic support was enlisted for Christian Missions. He heard Andrew Fuller tell what had been done by such men as Carey and Marshman ; and the grand idea of 'the conversion of the world,' once suggested, became a dominant thought, and the strong conviction deepened that Methodists, spiritual children of him who claimed 'the world as his parish' must not be the last to engage in the great work. Dawson expressed this thought, with a wonderful homely vigour, in the speech he delivered in 'the first public Wesleyan Missionary Meeting,' held in the Old Chapel, Leeds, on October 16, 1813. The presence of many faithful honoured ministers gave point to his description of 'our regular Ministry' as being 'truly of a Missionary kind.' Did not these men, he asked, sacrifice the comforts of a settled life, the pride of independence, the pleasures of social enjoyment, the dreams of wealth, the sweets of Christian friendship—for at the end of two years every tie must be broken, and they must move on—did they not leave father, mother, brothers, sisters, and embrace a wandering life, a humble, dependent station, arduous duties —and all that they might offer a ' full, free, present salvation' to the greatest possible number of their fellow sinners ? Were not these the sacrifices, was not this the spirit, of the Missionary ?

And could it be said these men had laboured in vain ? Had not widespread good resulted from their self-sacrificing toils in Great Britain, in the West Indies, in America ? But it needed not to go far afield ; close at hand was there not evidence how heaven could crown with blessing such 'missionary' zeal ?   'I look round on this congregation,' he went on passionately, indicating 'the dear fathers and honoured brethren' who sat near him—let us remember the presence of the noble, saintly Richard Watson, and many of his worthy compeers—'I ask you, have these men laboured in vain ?'   And winning an instant cry of 'No !' from hundreds of voices, he launched into a fervid appeal, urging on those who freely owned how richly they had profited by *missionary* effort in their own land, the duty of extending the same benefits to the distant heathen—bidding them not selfishly engross the riches of the Gospel to themselves.

The effect of this address, coming as it did after the audience had already been stirred and roused by orators as earnest though less audacious, is said to have been electrical. Stern, strong men—like the chairman, Mr. Thompson— melted into tears under its pathetic power, which we can only faintly indicate.   The speaker was soon in constant demand as a missionary advocate, and became closely associated with the cause, serving it perhaps more in his life than even Dr. Coke in his impressive devotion and death.   One drawback only to Dawson's many successes in this new field may be lightly indicated : his quaintness of speech, his dramatic boldness of action—natural and appropriate in him—the vivid flashes of his native humour, all these found would-be emulators who caricatured his effects, and introduced something ludicrous into their treatment of awe-inspiring themes.   Such is the testimony of an admiring contemporary of this great untaught orator.   He was too frankly original to be a safe model for commonplace men, and never less imitable than in his platform efforts on behalf of Missions.   For then he dared much, delighting to seize on topics of the day and turn them to spiritual account. Thus, when he was in his ripest maturity the rapid formation of railways was exciting general attention, and Dawson had his 'Railway' speech accordingly. 'The track was the world, the train was the Gospel, Jesus Christ was the chief director'—and so on. It needed all the practised skill and the genuine fervour of the speaker to keep this perilous allegory within reverent bounds ; even so his handling of it did not escape criticism.

He had too, at that time of wild political excitement when the Reform Bill had been thrown out by the House of Lords, a 'Reform Bill' speech, delivered at Bristol first— somewhat to the dismay of the dignified and prudent chairman of that meeting, James Montgomery, the Sheffield poet, who supplied a humorous description of the scene. Time and place were full of hazard ; the city was yet wild after recent riots, men's minds were stormy as the sea, and all political allusions were deemed unwise ; but the daring Yorkshireman took for his subject, 'the Bill, the whole Bill, nothing but the Bill,' and managed to go through it, clause by clause, imparting a distinctly religious meaning to every clause, and producing an effect almost overwhelming by his bold allegory ; yet doing all with a dexterity amid his seeming extravagance that never overstepped the limits of caution. It would have been impossible for any hearer to accuse the speaker of political bias.

Almost as impossible would it have been for any imitator to follow him safely on such lines.

The two famous speeches just cited belong to a much later period of Mr. Dawson's life than we have reached ; but already in 1814 he had given proof enough of the peculiar faculty for extracting profit from unlikely material of which these addresses are the best remembered examples—

proof enough of the gay fancy that was to sparkle in his 'Clock' speech, 'in which every wheel and spring and screw was emblematical of some part of the missionary agency'—proof enough of the prophetic hopefulness that breathed through his 'Telescope' speech, when he would survey the world through a 'perspective-glass' imaged by his half-clenched hand, and find new encouragement in every new field of effort to which he turned—and proof enough too of the rich, hallowed imagination that surviving hearers long loved to dwell upon in his 'Harvest Home.' All these later efforts of the farmer-preacher's genius had their foreshadowings in the animated addresses he gave at numerous meetings that followed close on that first memorable one at Leeds. His sphere of influence widened rapidly ; it was no longer limited to the West Riding or to Yorkshire ; it took in Cheshire, Lancashire, Durham, Northumberland. We have a lively picture of certain gentlemen 'from one of the principal towns in the kingdom,' coming post-haste to Leeds and Barnbow to secure his services in an emergency ; one of their leading speakers on a missionary occasion has failed them suddenly, who so likely as Dawson to fill the vacant place at the shortest notice ? Their chaise is seen with wonder at Barnbow—such vehicles rarely tempt the mud of its lanes—they have to seek the master in his fields, and find him bent over his spade, hedging and ditching. Were they doubtful of their man, their doubts had vanished at the first glance of the keen kindly face he uplifted to them.

They plead for the instant help of the ditcher. 'Go and help them he must, they cannot do without him,' and 'If it *must* be so, it *shall* be so,' he answers, after some modest hesitation. Promptly every arrangement is made, the master's shrill whistle calls his man to carry on the spade

work, exact directions are given for it, then the visitors must
taste the farmhouse fare of Barnbow; and anon they are
whirling away to Leeds, bearing with them their prize—a
shirt-sleeved labourer no more, but a yeoman clad in seemly
black, who 'keeps them alive all the way to Leeds' with
his sparkling talk, and who gives them even better help than
they looked for at their meeting in the far-distant town

THEY HAVE TO SEEK THE MASTER IN HIS FIELDS.—*p.* 70.

whither they were bound.   There is something in the little
incident quite typical of the position Dawson was long to
keep.   'Diligent in business,' even of the homeliest, ever
ready to put it aside for the nobler work when that called
for him, but not permitting the higher duty to mar the
discharge of the lower.

What the 'important town' of this story was we are not
told; but we find him in 1817-18 at Selby, at Darlington, at
Newcastle, at Sunderland, now touching with pathetic power

on the recent death of the Princess Charlotte, and now
winning the ear and heart of northern colliers as he
expounds the text, 'He brought me up out of the horrible
pit,' spiritualising after his wont the circumstances of their
calling.   And now he is in company with Dr. Adam Clarke,
sharing the cramped accommodation of a too full post-
chaise on the way from Chester to Liverpool, and enabling
his reverend companion to forget the miseries of the road
in the vivid interest roused by his conversation.   'Your
friend, Mr. Dawson, and myself talked all the way to Liverpool yesterday evening,' said Dr. Clarke to Robert Newton
the next day ; 'what an astonishing mind he has got !' and
the tribute from the accomplished scholar to the self-taught
genius was worth having.

Dawson found no Boswell to report his talk at full
length, but his biographer and others have preserved for us
many a saying, showing as much shrewd insight as kindliness, by which we may estimate what was his social
attractiveness.   He could criticise keenly without bitterness
and reprove without offending.

'You are one of the best takers of a likeness I ever met
with,' he said to a brother preacher.   'In drawing the
character of a sinner you do it to the life ; but on holding
the likeness up to the man, you invariably get him to laugh
at himself,' a fault how lightly touched ! and the hint was
not resented by the friend addressed.   And that was a good
reproof to the fault-finder who 'could get no good' from
the prayer-meeting held after Mr. Dawson had finished
preaching.   'I went up into the gallery,' he complained,
'and looked down on the people ; the sight of so much
disorder destroyed all the good previously received.'   'Ah,'
said Dawson, 'you mounted to the top of the house, and
on looking down your neighbour's chimney to see what sort

of a fire he kept, you got your eyes filled with smoke. Had you "entered by the door" and mingled with the family round the hearth, you would have enjoyed the benefit of the fire as well as they. Sir, *you have got the smoke in your eyes.*'

People delighted to hear this competent judge of his own grand art pronounce on the merits of other public speakers, and sometimes pressed too much for his opinion, as in the case of a certain minister from whose sermons little could be carried away for home meditation. What did Mr. Dawson think of him?

'I eat what I can, but pocket nothing,' was the reply by which he escaped their importunity—a definition as neat and crisp, but not so biting, as his description of an over-impressive style as being 'hot and heavy, like a tailor's goose.'

A calm and classic speaker, on the other hand, was as clearly characterised; his preaching 'was like the building of Solomon's temple—without noise, not so much as the sound of a hammer was heard.'

CHAPTER VI.

SOWING AND REAPING.

M R. DAWSON'S powers as a missionary advocate becoming daily more widely known, his engagements
multiplied fast ; and soon it was common for him to make
not less than a hundred evangelistic journeys in the year.
The 'service of steam' was in its unpromising childhood,
and could not as yet help him ; and since it was his wish to
economise as much as possible in the travelling expenses,
which were defrayed by those who sought his help, he
travelled rarely by the mail, often by the 'regular heavy
coaches,' and though extremity of weather sometimes drove
him to be an 'inside' passenger, commonly he sat outside,
in summer heat and winter cold, in frost and snow and
wind. Not unfrequently one of these journeys would consume three days. But the time spent on the road was not
wasted. He studied life and character here as elsewhere.

Sometimes quaint experiences befel him as he sat, a
sturdy, yeomanly figure, with nothing in dress or aspect to
distinguish him from other laymen, among the fellow-pas-
sengers who talked busily around him. We may call up
his image, square-shouldered, well muffled to the chin, his
wide-brimmed hat drawn low on his brows, his keen eyes
shining observant in the shadow, while the 'Manchester
coach,' on which his place is taken, rattles through Huddersfield streets, and a gentleman sitting by him says,
'There's a name I am always seeing! and I have heard a

great deal about the man. Do you know anything about him ?'

The question is not addressed to Dawson, who catches sight of his own name on some large posters that advertise the occasional sermons he preached a few days ago in Huddersfield. He hears another passenger answer :

' I heard him once several years ago ; I am not likely to forget the sermon or the text. He is not a regular preacher among the Methodists, they tell me ; he is a thorough farmer, living at home with his mother. But he is an extraordinary man.'

'Not so polished, I suppose, as the Rev. Robert Newton,' quoth the first speaker ; 'but he may do very well for the lower classes.' And turning to the silent Dawson, he enquired :

' You know Leeds and its neighbourhood, perhaps ? Ah, you do ! Have you heard the preacher we are speaking of ? What do you think of him ?'

' I have heard him—yes,' says Dawson rather drily ; ' but I must say I think him overrated by being styled an " extraordinary man." '

There was an instant outcry. ' He may be unlearned ; he must ; but see how popular he is, what immense congregations he draws !'

' Yes,' struck in the other ; ' if there were not extraordinary natural powers, and if he were not a good speaker also, how could an illiterate man such as he is produce such amazing effects ?'

Dawson listened in modest silence and inward amusement. But now Huddersfield was left behind ; the ascent of Stanedge began, and the outside passengers alighted to make it on foot. He held himself a little aloof from his travelling companions as they climbed the slope, unwilling to be recognised by *him* who had once been a hearer of his own.

' I am glad,' ran his musings, ' that they think I can be useful to the poor ; they need help the most. Unlearned, illiterate ! they are right, it is what I am. But I have extraordinary gifts ! then God give me grace to use them to His glory. I hope the gentleman will not find out who I am ; it might make him uneasy. But I am stouter than I was, and not dressed for the pulpit ; I think he will not know me.'

His hope was fulfilled. He mounted the coach again, heard himself discussed once more in free and friendly fashion, and parted from his fellow-travellers in Manchester without their finding out who had listened to their criticisms. He was armed too strong in humility for these to hurt him ; but they could profit him, showing whether he had attained or not to his own high ideal of the right style and aim of preaching.

' Bring your sermons,' he wrote to a young beginner ; ' and every sentence in them, to this touch-stone—" Will this glorify God, and, especially, edify the people ? Shall I leave my hearers admiring my Lord, and hating sin, and forgetting myself ? " . . . Gospel truth is a sovereign, and that of no common order ; and, I readily grant, preaching is the carriage in which he rides. I confess, too, that I do not like to see him ride in a common, paltry cart of bad grammar, low metaphor, and vulgar dialect. His majesty is worthy of a better vehicle than the head and heart and hands of men ever made. But still I should not like to see a preacher turning the attention of the crowd to the composition, the painting, and the gilding of the chariot so as to lose sight of the monarch who rides in it—or should ride in it.'

The manly simplicity which he recommended marked his own style ; if the choice lay between a strong plain word and one more refined and more obscure, he never hesitated ; and it was this directness and vigour that gave him much of his power—the power to win souls for Christ, which alone he coveted. 'He would have been spoiled by an academical education,' said the Rev. J. A. James ; and if we may question this, remembering that such an education did not 'spoil' the plain speech of Wesley, it is at least not doubtful that Dawson's assiduous self-culture stood him in good stead, for his long and intimate acquaintance with the old Puritans had imparted to his manner of expressing himself something of that quaint homeliness which is farthest from vulgarity. He was not unaware of this, and the charge of 'illiteracy' passed him by lightly, while the testimony to his soul-winning eloquence cheered him.

Not always were his own powers the theme of the way-side talk from which he gathered useful hints. Making one of the 'six insides' of a coach running between Leeds and Halifax, he heard a lady and gentleman discussing other 'popular preachers,' and the fair critic pronouncing authoritatively on the merits of this minister and that. Mr. Watson had the honour of her approval. 'He never exhausts a figure ; I would go ten miles to hear him.' Edward Irving, then at the height of his fame, displeased by the ambitious novelty of his pulpit style; another preacher 'never suggests a new thought,' and yet another was too fanciful. 'His imagination is like a colt turned loose into a field.' Dawson listened and remembered. He well knew that he himself was sometimes in peril from the over-richness of his pictorial imagination ; but his was not the name that incurred the lady's scornful dispraise. Curiously it happened that not long after, in a large party, he met the gentleman in question, who was exercising his wit at the expense of his brethren in the ministry there present. 'Your fancy runs away with you,' was the burden of his mocking criticism of one in particular, and he included William Dawson in the jest. The temptation was irresistible ; Dawson must gravely reply that an unbridled fancy was indeed an evil, hurtful to a preacher's usefulness; and then he rehearsed some part of the conversation to which he had listened a few days before, giving due prominence to that too apt comparison of his critic's imagination to a colt wildly gambolling in a field· Silence, and a little confusion, fell on the incautious jester, and the other victim of his raillery said softly to Dawson : ' This *colt* has trodden on both of us, but we shall not be hurt ; like most young horses turned out to grass, he is without shoes."

Was this one of the occasions when Dawson's sensitive conscience rebuked him for indulgence in ' levity ' ? Scarcely so ; the rebuke he had administered was needed, and it had been given in no unkindly spirit ; sharply though it was felt at the moment, we may believe it would be of profit.

Yet another travelling adventure may for a moment arrest our attention. Taking his place outside a coach, Dawson finds beside him a youth in sailor's dress, who seems light-hearted and gay, full of song and jest and mirth-moving story ; open-handed he is, and in true sailor fashion flings his money to every passing beggar, and is anxious to treat his companions at every stopping-place. There is a sort of refinement about his look and speech ; very inoffensive are his witty sayings, however wild. Presently it comes out that he has been college-bred, and can adorn his talk with scraps of Virgil's verse. Dawson's interest is awakened, and gently he tries to turn the conversation to matters of deeper moment; he speaks of the work of man's redemption, of the need for a Saviour.

'Oh, there is no Redeemer mentioned in the Old Testament!' says the youth.

'What! not in the Book of Job?' asks Dawson.

'Not *certainly*,' replies the sailor-lad; 'the word you translate, *Redeemer*, in the famous passage: "I know that my Redeemer liveth," has another meaning also—it can mean "an avenger,"' and having quoted the Hebrew term, he seems to think the whole great question of the atonement disposed of.

'Will you have a song?' he says, turning to the other passengers. He begins to chant a sort of ballad on a boating accident that happened some years before, on the river Ouse, below York; but his clear voice grows husky as he reaches the verse that tells how the boat was swept over a lock, and how one of its boyish crew perished. The song ceases.

'I was there myself,' he says; 'it was my friend who was drowned,' and it proved that he had been one of the scholars of a 'Socinian Seminary' in the ancient cathedral city when the disaster took place. His curious theological lore, so strange in a sailor, was accounted for.

Poor boy! he had lavished away all his money before the journey's end was reached, and though he refused to be 'treated,' he was not unwilling to share Dawson's travelling provision, which was delicately offered him. Touched and softened, he said, as they drew near Birmingham:

'My father's house is very near this place; to-night I shall be either *shut in* or *shut out*. If shut in,'—he glanced from his own rough jacket to Dawson's seemly broadcloth— 'well! I may be as well clad as a Methodist parson. To-night will settle all.'

Have you broken your mother's heart, poor youth ? have you been sent from home, have you fled from it ? and will the door open for you ? thought Dawson sadly. His wayward fellow-passenger swung himself down from the coach and went his way ; but often the phrase '*shut in* my father's house, or *shut out* from it,' recurred to William Dawson's memory, and in preaching he would refer to the wanderer and to others as widely astray who yet might be *shut into* their Father's house above. 'This night may settle all.' The incident became a powerful allegory in his hands, and once when he had made most touching use of it a lady awaited him after the service to say, ' I know the young man you spoke of—I know his family. You will be glad to learn that he was not shut out that night—he was shut in.'

The incident just cited shows us William Dawson ready to take any fitting opportunity of saying a word for his Master ; indeed, he was always on the alert, as one of his favourite authors has it, ' to gather up every fragment, scrap, and shred of time,' and use it for the glory of God. As he rode to and from Leeds, he was not so absorbed in the business that took him there but that he could have a quick eye to the chances of serving some better end. Very often he met on his way a miller's man, well known to him as having once chosen the better part, and then fallen back into godless ways, in which he was wretched.

' Have you joined the regiment again, John ? ' was the greeting this poor fellow would hear, as Dawson checked his horse to hail him ; and, well understanding what was meant, John would answer, ' Nay, master, not yet.'

Question and answer would be followed by some kind warning word ; but the backslider did not retrace his downward steps, until one day Dawson said a sharper thing. Fixing his penetrating glance on him, he demanded : ' Do you know what you are? You are a deserter from God and truth. And as a deserter, you will have to be either *whipt* or *shot!*' With that word he left him, but John remained persuaded that some very heavy punishment was in store for him. Was it bodily suffering? Was it endless misery? He dared not face either prospect; and it was not long before the glad news reached William Dawson that

VERY OFTEN HE MET ON HIS WAY A MILLER'S MAN.—*p.* 80.

this wandering soul had found its way back to God and goodness, and was living in the light of forgiveness and peace.

Tracts, those silent preachers, were always a part of Dawson's travelling equipment; but he would not scatter them indiscriminately, offering them only to wayfarers who seemed to need such teachers. One of his booklets fell into the hands of a man who could not read, and who,

7

turning over the printed paper with suspicion and fear, ran after the giver in breathless haste. 'Is it a summons you've served on me?' he panted out. 'A summons!' repeated Dawson; 'ah, yes! but not the sort you're thinking of. It is a summons to pay the debt you owe to God, not to man —and it is yourself you owe to Him, your life and soul and all you are;' and with his own surprising readiness he followed out the hint so strangely given, to the benefit of his astonished hearer, whom he urged also, on parting, to acquaint himself with the art of reading, which might save him from more damaging mistakes than that which he had just made.

We might multiply indefinitely such instances of the prompt and forcible counsel he could give, fitted to all the varieties of character with which he now was made acquainted : a few must suffice.

'I am poor; I have few gifts; what can my feeble efforts be worth?' complained some drooping Little-Faith in his presence,

'Poor, are you, and can do nothing?' was the reply. 'Nay, with the grace of God in your heart, you can do something! Let us say you are no better than a farthing candle. Well, even a farthing candle can give light to a beggar. A farthing candle, and can do nothing! Yes, you can set a town on fire—nay, you can set a world on fire! Some of the first public speakers were probably lighted by the meanest taper.' There was hope and life in the energetic words. He had others, more biting, at the service of one who evidently thought only of this world.

'Imagine yourself,' he would say, 'in a room that is strewed with money—old, worn copper coins, and new sovereigns. What would you think of a man who is free to come in and help himself, and you see him anxiously picking

up the defaced and dirty farthings, loading himself with
them, and the bright new coined gold, where you may see
the image and superscription of the King, he scorns to
gather it! That is what a worldling does—he spends his
whole time in picking up mere trifles; he neglects the
"gold tried in the fire." If he would but take the sovereigns

'IS IT A SUMMONS YOU'VE SERVED ON ME?'—*p.* 82.

instead, he would have the farthings *in* the sovereigns.
We have the Redeemer's word for it, that if we "seek first
the Kingdom of God and His righteousness, all these
things shall be added unto us" that the men of this world
are so eager about.'

· But his most stinging rebuke was reserved for those who
presumed on his well-known love of humorous talk to speak
with 'light irreverence' on themes not fit for mirth. One

who **had** no pretensions to piety, after listening to the conversation of some religious friends with Mr. Dawson, remarked :

'I shall be turning serious, too, one of these days ; and then I will have a sale of my goods ; I'll sell off all my stock of sins by public auction.'

'You will find no buyer for the stuff,' said Dawson, sternly. 'The devil will give no price for it—it is his already ; God will have nothing to do with it—He hates it ; men need it not, for they will find they have enough of their own without it.' It was no sound jest, to his mind, when a fool made a mock of sin ; and the unseasonable jester was put to silence and to shame in his presence.

Such, and so consistent in his bearing amid the larger society now open to him, was the William Dawson who was in ever-increasing request, and dangerously popular, from one end of England to the other. We may note one more famous sermon amid the many he delivered in the years from 1817 to 1824—his first at Sunderland, addressed to a congregation of sailors. Well experienced in ploughing the land, he had little practical knowledge of their ways and customs who plough the deep ; but the kind host who entertained him spent some hours showing him the town, and exhibited in particular the life-boat, which fixed Mr. Dawson's attention. He had found his clue. Preaching in the evening, he set before his sailor hearers a vivid picture of a shipwreck as seen from the shore ; the wind raging thunderously, and the thunder of the waves answering as they rose in liquid mountains and sank in awful hollows, while the doomed ship is driven on to its fate. Wives, children, friends stand on the beach, helpless spectators ; 'My brother is lost—my father is there,' cries one and another, despairing, as the vessel strikes, shivers, and is broken on the rocks. Still some survivors cling to the wreck that, beaten to pieces in the surf, is on the point of disappearing in the foaming, roaring chaos. 'What is to be done now?—all is going—going for ever!' cries the preacher. 'What is to be done?' comes an answering shout from a sailor in the midst of the congregation; 'why, launch the life-boat!'

A dead hush followed that cry; then a shudder of excitement ran through the assembly; and the preacher availed himself at once of the hint given. He painted man as lost in the general shipwreck of human nature—sure to plunge into the gulf of eternal destruction—sure to lose sight of pious father, mother, brother, and sister, who vainly stretch out their hands to him—if he rejects the one means of escape and salvation, the Life-Boat of heaven! And what a sea of terrors is that which will then engulf him—what waves of fire raised to mountain height by the winds of eternity! 'Blessed be God!' he said, taking the Bible into his hands, 'though there is no life-boat in hell, we have one here! Come into the Life-Boat, and you shall not be destroyed with that everlasting destruction; you shall not sink into the raging waves of sin; you shall land safe on the shores of heaven!' Then with all the power of his touching eloquence he dwelt on the love and the almighty greatness of the Saviour, Himself the Author and the Way of life, and besought his hearers to come to *Him* who alone could save them. His words went straight home; the seamen understood and answered to his appeals. Many a sailor that night was rescued from the gulfs of sin into which he had been sinking; and for years after they loved to talk of what they called 'The Life-Boat Sermon.'

'If Methodism does not make men into *parsons*, it

certainly converts them into *clerks*; for they are responding
" Amen ! " " Glory be to God ! " wherever we go,' said
William Dawson once, with cheerful satisfaction. Few
preachers, even among his Methodist brethren, can have
called out so many involuntary responses, like that which
was wrung from the eager sailor—tributes to his rare power
of *acting* a scene so as to make his hearers see what he saw.
If he were dwelling on that parable of parables, the Prodigal
Son, he would draw to the life the ragged, weary, footsore
wretch limping slowly homeward, coming nearer and nearer
till, looking towards the door, he exclaimed, 'Yonder he
comes, slip-shod ! make way—make way, there ! ' and many
among the hearers started up and turned round, asking with
eager eyes, 'Where is he ? ' so completely had the preacher's
imagination imposed itself on them for reality. But little
would he have prized successes like these if he had not been
able to gain successes far more precious through them. If
he called up the image of that trembling penitent, it was
that he might win others, who had gone astray, to leave 'the
far country ' and its unsatisfying husks, fit only for swine,
and to seek their Father's house and its ready welcome. If
he painted in darker colours the weird haunt of the witch of
Endor and its grim tenant till men started and looked down,
expecting to see an awful shape arising in their midst, it was
that he might with greater power warn those who heard
against such godless despair as that of Saul.

Sometimes he feared that he failed in this higher aim.
'My heart sinks at times,' he wrote to a sympathising friend,
'when I consider that I range about the country to such an
extent, and get so little game ; that I traverse such an extent
of ocean, and catch so little fish ! Oh, for wisdom to win
souls ! ' But there were not wanting testimonies to the
immediate good done by his preaching—such testimonies

as greatly cheered him. One person would write and say, pleading for a second visit:

'If Mr. Dawson will come again to this place, he will have the pleasure of seeing a very respectable man who was —till he heard him when last in the neighbourhood—a poor, degraded, drunken backslider, and had been such for years. He gladly confesses that Mr. Dawson was, in the Lord's hand, the instrument of his conversion.'

Another, addressing the preacher by letter, said, 'I have heard you preach on the duty of Restitution. Help me to fulfil it! In company with others, I stole a large sum years ago. The owners I cannot now find; take the money I send, it represents my guilty gains. Spend it for me in the cause of God! thus only I can make restitution.'

And yet another would say: 'You were preaching at Newcastle to an overflowing congregation; the very doorway was crowded with listeners. Two colliers were passing, and one of them, a professed deist, said to the other, "Let us hear what this fellow is bawling about," and they stood still to hearken. Presently the other said, "Come, let us go." "Nay, I will hear him out," said the unbeliever. Soon he was touched to the heart; he was convinced of his sin and his danger; his professed scepticism vanished, and he sought and found pardon and peace — only just in time! A fortnight after there was a fall of roof in the pit where he was working, and he was crushed to death. Happy for him that he had heard God speak to him through *you* !'

Many such cases were brought to the preacher's knowledge, but still better results of his work were noted by others. He came to a town, he preached, he went away; but he left behind him a little army of workers who had caught the flame of his zeal and carried on the work he had begun. 'He drew them to God, not only to himself; he left them with a relish for the ministry of others as well as his own,' so that his advent was often the signal for a true and lasting revival of religious activities in the places he visited.

CHAPTER VII.

PREACHER AND PHILANTHROPIST.

THE year 1824 was made sadly memorable to Mr. Dawson. In its earliest months his venerable mother was suffering already from the complaint that proved fatal to her, and she lingered on, frail and feeble, only till July. For more than forty years the mother and son had housed together, loving and beloved; and very bitterly was the separation felt.

Mrs. Dawson had not been one who would hold back her 'Willy' from the work that God had given him. It was only when she was very feeble and broken down with sickness that he had to say, 'I have been much from home lately, and my mother is timorous about my leaving again.' It seemed at first as if the freedom of his movements would suffer from her departure. Safely had his heart trusted in her, and in the dear sister who was trained up in her ways and who succeeded to her household cares. But this sister left his house for one of her own, and, doubly deprived, William Dawson began to fear he could not with prudence spend so much time in 'running about the country.' Would it be right to leave his brother and his home to the care of servants only? must not such separations be very rare?

'Many say to me, "Take a wife," but those who *have* wives say, that if I had one she would never consent that I should neglect home as much as I have done; so that a wife would, in this case, be a stone to my foot, and I could not fly to preach occasional sermons, to beg for Sunday-schools, or to plead for missions.' So, with a half-humorous sadness, Dawson wrote when his loss was more than a year old. Judging marriage, however untruly, to be a very desperate remedy for his difficulty, he did not seek help that way, choosing to remain wedded to his work. In some fashion the apprehended hindrance to that work was set aside, and his public engagements multiplied instead of lessening. He found it needful to keep free the latter part of July, and the whole of August and of October in each year. Hay-harvest, corn-harvest, and seed-time must not be broken in upon by this 'Yorkshire farmer,' but from January to July, and in the closing months of the year, his services were in constant request—so much so that it was necessary for his arrangements to be made twelve months in advance ; and with Sabbath duties in his own circuit, fully half his time was devoted to the work of the Kingdom, which was its own reward, but which imposed heavy toil in farm and field on him when he was at home. Freely he gave and nobly ; ready to count all things lost for Christ's sake, and to work incessantly, week in and week out, that he might proclaim Him ; and though for many a year his was little better than a hand-to-mouth existence, he was never allowed to suffer the loss of any good thing, however often that loss was threatened.

Without pretending to the character of an author, William Dawson yet contrived to find a little time for some modest efforts at composition, in short memoirs of various pious friends, that duly appeared in *The Wesleyan Methodist Magazine* ; but the year 1826 brought him a task of this kind which he could not discharge alone. One whom he fondly called 'my friend, my brother, nay, my child,' the Rev. David Stoner, son of a dear friend at Barwick, and an early convert of Dawson's own ministry, was taken from a life of great usefulness in his early prime ; and his sorrowing friend rendered material help in compiling the Memoir which was prefixed to Stoner's *Diary and Correspondence*, by Dr. (then Mr.) Hannah, and which was signed by both authors. Inexpert at such work, William Dawson found a more congenial way of witnessing to the excellences of his much-loved fellow worker, in preaching funeral discourses on the occasion of his death at many places where David Stoner was personally known.

Those who heard long remembered the 'overpowering eloquence' of one of these addresses. He spoke of the departed saint as a herald of the Gospel, now lying low in death, 'the trumpet fallen from his hand,' which had given no uncertain sound, when with clarion-blast he summoned hundreds to rally round the Banner of the Cross, or pealed forth the joyful note announcing the Year of Jubilee. ' Fain would I take up his fallen trumpet,' he cried, ' and sound an alarm to the poor backslider once roused from lethargy by his voice, but now prostrate again. What meanest thou, O sleeper? Start at once upon thy feet ! Let his death be thy life ; let his happy spirit hear in heaven that the prodigal, who has left his Father's house, is returning to it !' Then, dwelling on the short life of which two-thirds had been spent in God's service, he made passionate appeal to his younger hearers to emulate that devotion. ' His day was short, but well filled up. His work is done, the trumpet has dropped from his hand. Is there no young man willing to take it up ?' he asked with touching earnestness, when with dramatic action he had seemed to ' sound an alarm,' with full, rich tones, the Gospel message that he pealed forth fading and dying away upon the ear in fainter accents till it ceased—for the trumpeter himself had fallen ! And one young man's heart answered to the call, and was

moved to the resolve of undertaking the duty from which, in
timid self-distrust, he had long been shrinking.

'If Mr. Dawson,' said one who knew both men, 'had
wrought no other good effect than that of working decision
in the mind of Samuel Entwisle, his labour had not been in
vain in the Lord.' For it was a beautiful soul into which
light and joy came with that clarion-call of the preacher who
sometimes thought very meanly of his own power to do
good. 'Made perfect in a short time,' this young evangelist
soon in his turn passed to a brighter world, but his brief
life could never have left so inspiring a memory as it did
had it not been for that inspiring sermon, which, said one
who listened, 'will be remembered to the latest hour of its
last surviving hearer.'

It was very characteristic of William Dawson thus to
turn to holy use, and to the profit of the Church bereaved
of a zealous worker, the death which was a great personal
grief to himself. Some other distresses, in which the wide-
ness of his sympathies involved him, could not be so utilised ;
they seemed barren evils, and they troubled him the more.
Such were the yet unforgotten dissensions which shook the
Leeds Society during 1827-28, and caused the immediate
loss of some hundreds of members, the matter in dispute
being so trivial-seeming as the erection of an organ in
Brunswick Chapel. 'It has cost me more waking and
aching hours than anything that ever happened to me,'
wrote he, who, without being implicated in the contention,
watched it most anxiously ; but soon his best hope was that
'the breach might spread no further,' and that, through the
wise action of Conference, 'the broken limb might become
sounder and stronger than before the fracture.' Loving-
hearted and loyal, he never willingly referred to the strife
when it was ended, believing and hoping that many who

had withdrawn themselves in hasty anger might yet be won back.

Love of country was closely blended with zeal for God in William Dawson's mind ; and only less than the grief which pierced him when he saw wrath and strife among Christians was that with which he regarded the many social wrongs that were rife in his dear England. There was great, and, as he believed, unnecessary commercial depression, which he traced to 'the curse of England—unscriptural speculation,' a sin, in his judgment, calling for stronger denunciation than common betting and gambling. And, living in the midst of one great manufacturing district, and a frequent visitor to others, he saw and heard many things that convinced him of deep evils connected with the factory system of that day, with its long, exhausting hours and its employment of little children, 'early wakened out of sleep in the morning—their ears stunned with the monotonous buzz, and their eyes confounded with the incessant whirl of the wheels of the factory all the day—and then returning home weary and exhausted in the evening—and this for six days out of seven in the week !' So, in humble prose that recalls the glowing verse of Elizabeth Barrett Browning, he wrote of these child-martyrs, in a public letter, addressed to 'his friend M. T. Sadler, Esq., M.P.,' who, in concert with many gentlemen and with not a few large-hearted mill-owners, was endeavouring to bring about that 'shortening of the hours of labour in factories' which the Ten Hours Bill finally accomplished. This letter, and another addressed to the chairman of a meeting at Halifax convoked in aid of the same object, are still worthy of study. Their writer takes his stand on high ground, choosing to dwell on the grievous moral injury inflicted on child and woman by the trade customs that required mill-work, beginning with very infancy, to be kept up during not less than eleven and a half hours of each working day, as the little one grew into the maturity when longer tasks would be exacted. What chance had these weary toilers of acquiring 'divine or useful knowledge'? Only the Sunday-school stood in the gap; and its zealous workers, withdrawing themselves from public worship, found five hours of every Sabbath too short for teaching mere reading and writing and a little Scripture truth to the dazed, exhausted scholars they could collect. The evil results of the system to such girl-workers as lived into womanhood were too apparent. Home-training there could hardly be; fatherly and motherly lessons in piety, virtue, and thrift were all but impossible; and the consequent degrading ignorance of those who should have become sweet and serviceable house-mothers led them too often into vices that destroyed happiness and usefulness and character. What then was the prospect for the next generation?

Was it said that any humane reform would destroy England's manufacturing greatness? If our national prosperity could only be bought by the physical, mental, moral degradation of our people, surely the doom prophesied for Egypt would come on England; 'it shall be the basest of the nations; . . . God will diminish it, and it shall no more rule among the nations.'

But this Christian man believed in a happier solution of the problem. He would fain see employer and employed standing to each other as father and children, each desiring and promoting the welfare of the other, bound together by 'the threefold cord of affection, obligation, and dependence.' Dare we say this could not be? Nay, he will hope that English masters and English labourers will yet adopt the Cornish motto 'One and all,' and dealing justly and lovingly with each other, will find that their interests need not and do not clash ! Dawson's political economy was that of 'his Master, Jesus'; its principles were founded on the Great Commandments. Well assured he was that the man who loved God with heart and soul and mind, and his neighbour as himself, would not fail to do to all men whatsoever things he would that they should do to him ! 'If masters and servants fully act on *these* principles, we shall not want legal enactments to oblige either party to do that which is lawful and right'; and not only one set of evils, but many, would pass away like mist.

That special reform for which Dawson pleaded has long since been accomplished, without any of the predicted 'ruin' to the special industry concerned. But, could he live and speak in his England to-day, he would more emphatically re-affirm the grand principles on which he saw that the right relations between master and servant, capital and labour, should be founded; his arm would be nerved 'to give another blow to the rivet of humanity, justice and truth—to clench more firmly the nail that binds society together, and that makes us helpers of each other's interests, from the sovereign to the meanest subject.' The words, spoken sixty years ago, are not out of date yet; 'legal enactments' like that by which Dawson and his friends were fain to seek the amendment of the factory system, have been multiplied to protect man against man; and still thousands of our countrymen do not understand, as did this plain 'Yorkshire farmer,' how the law of Christ is the perfect law of liberty, for nations as for individuals.

The keen interest that William Dawson took in public questions such as these, was free from 'party and political feeling,' and never interfered with his usefulness as a preacher. How, indeed, could he better serve every class of his countrymen than by publishing among them the good news of salvation from sin, and teaching them love to God and love to man? So we find him busier than ever in his special work during the troubled years that preceded and followed the accession of William IV. in 1830. They brought him his own share of sorrows in the loss of dear friends; among these was Samuel Hick, 'the Village Blacksmith,' whose deathbed he visited and comforted, and whose temporal concerns he settled; his deep respect for that humble, quaint, fine-spirited Christian was shown in many ways; he attended his funeral, preached two memorial sermons on his death, and wrote a brief account of him for *The Wesleyan Methodist Magazine*; while he did not forget to care for Samuel's widow as long as she lived; some of the profits of the larger memoir of her husband, by Mr. Everett, were set aside for her benefit by the author, and transmitted to her through Dawson's hands.

We may note that this was only one of many instances in which the high opinion that people entertained of William Dawson's integrity and ability brought on him various trusteeships that made large demands on his time; but he never failed in any of these obligations, burdensome as they sometimes proved.

His own affairs gave him some trouble; times and seasons were bad, his farm was poor and did not pay, three valuable horses died of distemper at one time; and a generous friend offered him a better farm, near Newcastle, 'at any rent you like to pay,' ran the proposal, which, however, he would not accept. 'I will not take advantage of your kindness while I have any hopes of improvement here,' said he; 'perhaps I should be leaving my providential place.' And years did bring improvement, so that he could say, 'I am as comfortable in my farm as I need be.'

One calamitous accident caused him deep distress. He

was preaching occasional sermons at Heckmondwike in the April of 1829, and as usual the chapel was crowded to excess; some person was pushed against a stove-pipe, which noisily gave way under his weight, and instantly a panic arose. 'The chapel is falling,' shrieked some one; there was a wild rush to the doors, cries, confusion; five persons were either crushed or trampled to death, and another so injured as to die the next day. The spectacle of this frightful tumult, the knowledge of its fatal results, made the most painful impression on the preacher. He could not be induced to revisit Heckmondwike until more than eight years had elapsed. What had happened there once might happen again under similar circumstances. It is a little surprising, indeed, considering the crowds always attracted by his preaching, and the excitement it generally produced, that this fatality stands alone in his story. That quick and sparkling humour which often relieved the solemnity of his utterances was doubtless useful in many instances, lessening the almost painful tension of the nerves, that might have had like disastrous results; no less serviceable would be the variety that he knew how to introduce by his use of hymns. He chose these with much care, and could draw great advantage from the old Methodist way of singing two lines at a time as they were given out from the pulpit. When the lines just sung had been—

> ' True, 'tis a strait and thorny road,
>   And mortal spirits tire and faint,'

he paused to say, 'Why do they tire? Because the way is " strait and thorny"? Nay,—

> ' " But they forget the mighty God,
>   That feeds the strength of every saint," '

thus impressing the true teaching of the hymn on the minds

8

of those who sang, yet avoiding any sense of interruption. Again, he had chosen the grand hymn beginning—

> ' Jesu, Thy blood and righteousness
> My beauty are, my glorious dress,'

and before giving out the last verse he said : ' I have often been struck with the language of the minister in the Communion service, when he says, " Lift up your hearts," and the people respond, " We lift them up unto the Lord " ; the minister strikes in, " Let us give thanks unto our Lord God " ; the people respond, " It is meet and right so to do," and the minister closes in with, " It is very meet, right, and our bounden duty, that we should at all times, and in all places, give thanks unto Thee, O Lord, holy Father, almighty and everlasting God ! " ' Then looking round the congregation, he lifted up his voice to say with fire, ' " Lift up your hearts "—yea, let the whole congregation repeat, " We lift them up unto the Lord," ' and instantly announced—

> ' Thou God of power, Thou God of love,
> Let the whole world Thy mercy prove !
> Now let Thy word o'er all prevail ;
> Now take the spoils of death and hell.'

The power of sound increased at once fourfold—a grand burst of congregational singing filled the place, seeming to bear up every soul on wings of devotion ; and in the prayer that immediately followed the emphatic responses of the people showed how thoroughly they had been aroused to take their right interest in the service.

In like manner he prefaced the words, ' See all your sins on Jesus laid,' by pausing to read from the sixth chapter of the Apocalypse the invitation so often repeated to 'Come and see' one mysterious terror after another. 'But I do not now ask you,' he said, 'to come and see the preacher, to come and hear a voice of thunder—come and see yourselves, your sins, your Saviour! "Come and see"—what?' And with sparkling eyes and eloquent expression he poured forth the words—-

> '*See* all your sins on Jesus laid !
> The Lamb of God was slain ;
> His soul was once an offering made
> For every soul of man !'

words instantly taken up by the congregation with a fervour that showed how their mind's eye had indeed been fixed on their suffering Saviour.

It was a quainter use that he made of a hymn-verse, when he chose to liken the enemy of souls to an idiot-lad who was found hard at work trying to 'rub out the name' from a brass door-plate. 'The poor boy did not know that the harder he rubbed the brighter it shone. So is it,' added Dawson, 'with Satan; he would fain obliteratet he word of God from the memory, the understanding, the heart. But his toil is vain ;

> 'Engraved as in eternal brass
> The mighty promise shines ;
> Nor can the powers of darkness rase
> Those everlasting lines.'

Then, as if he saw the fiend at his fruitless toil, he cried, 'Rub! yes, rub! all is in vain ; the evidence only grows brighter for the attempt; because the Lord—yes, of Him it may be said—

> 'His hand hath writ the sacred word
> With an immortal pen.'

'There was great inequality in his preaching,' said one who knew and admired Mr. Dawson ; how indeed could it be otherwise with a man who did not calculate his effects beforehand, and whose eloquence was so much the spontaneous expression of a rich, irregular genius, springing up

like a fiery fountain from the depths of his glowing heart as
its strong pulse-play dictated? So there would sometimes
be hesitation and difficulty before he could find words that
would best set forth a new-sprung thought, and sometimes
there would be something strange and startling in the action
by which he would illustrate it; but to those who can
remember him he is, notwithstanding, 'the prince of old
preachers.' Shall we look on him as he appeared after very
many years of hard toil had passed over his head?
He is massive in form, he moves with the rolling gait
of a true son of the soil; all eyes are caught by
his appearance as he mounts the pulpit stairs. Keen, glowing eyes shine under his overhanging eyebrows; false hair,
which he will often adjust with both hands as he speaks,
half hides his broad, lofty, prominent forehead. This
nervous trick of meddling with his ill-fitting wig is the subject of some mirth for him and his friends, but that, and
everything else remarkable in his aspect, is forgotten as he
warms to his subject; the interest of his words overpowers
all. For now he is dwelling on the grand uniformity which
marks the experience of all God's children. 'They have all
one tale to tell,' says he; 'let us call some of them up to tell
it!' And first he utters the name of a famous minister,
noted for his great learning, and well-known to him and his
hearers. 'Adam Clarke! you who can speak sixteen lan-
guages, tell us about your conversion.' And the great
doctor, by the lips of the preacher, speaks of humble peni-
tence, patient waiting on God, blissful forgiveness for
Christ's sake. Then the call is: 'Barnabas Shaw! you
are a Missionary; some of your African converts can speak
in a love-feast; what do they say?' In their broken
English those converted savages stammer forth a tale
just like the learned doctor's. 'Now,' goes on the preacher,

'you have had a great revival here. One of you drunkards and swearers that were saved, tell us how it was with *you*.' And the rough voice of the conquered English rebel tells in trembling tones how *he*, who seemed lost for ever, has been rescued by the Almighty Saviour—and still it is the same story! 'Now,' questions the preacher, 'what does this king say? "I waited patiently for the Lord, and He inclined unto me and heard my cry. He brought me up out of the horrible pit."' Ah, what pit more horrible than that where a sinner lies in the darkness of a guilty conscience? The king knew what it was to lie in that pit, and for him there was no way of escape but the one way that all whom we have heard speak have taken.

'See,' cries the speaker, pointing, 'see the chain that hangs down into the black hopeless pit! It reaches down very near to hell—and not only up to the gate of Heaven, but to the very Throne! See the links of that chain—one is God's love, one His mercy, one His grace, one His truth—they are past counting; but every link is strong with heaven's strength—the chain is long enough and strong enough; there it hangs within thy very reach—seize it, poor despairing sinner, cling to it; it will lift thee out of the pit. Do not fear to trust it; see, above thee, all these saints of God who have risen, clinging to this chain! But refuse to trust thyself to it, let it pass out of thy reach, and thou art lost for ever!'

In all such bold impersonations and such vivid picturings there was risk; they might sometimes come very near the line where the sublime merges into something very different, yet they never overpassed it; so intense was the solemnity of the preacher's manner, so fervent his desire to deliver fully the message of salvation to perishing souls, that they might hear and live.

CHAPTER VIII.

DARK DAYS AND BRIGHT DAYS.

THE years which saw William Dawson anxious to strike one blow on behalf of the victims of the factory system were dark with many other clouds threatening the welfare of England. Strange crimes were abroad in the land ; here, there, from this rick-yard and that, flames shot up fiercely in the dead of night, telling how the garnered grain and hay were burning in fires wilfully kindled, and the hopes of the farmer and the food of man and beast were crumbling into ashes together. Insane mischief, that could not profit its ignorant, half-starved perpetrators or feed their hunger ! and there were murders, too, of rare brutality, the victims being stupefied with drink and drugs, and then drowned while still unconscious. In his correspondence with that much-prized friend, the Rev. T. Galland, Dawson dwelt mournfully on these things ; he saw something fiend-like in them. 'A spirit is let loose on the souls of men,' said he, 'by which they commit acts of iniquity and mischief such as were never heard of or read of since the world stood.' At this very time, also, the cholera first spread its black wings over England and struck down its thousands. Dawson, in pursuance of his sacred work, went to Newcastle and its neighbourhood, where the plague was busy ; he was appalled at its ravages, and, though fearless on his own account, was distressed to see that no religious awe was kindled by this new calamity among the godless, that thieves were busy as ever, even among the crowds at the door of the chapel where he preached!

The months ran on, and in August the grim pestilence walked abroad in Little Barwick; three-fourths of those who were stricken died, and the threatening weather made him sigh, 'A dark appearance for harvest!' But fearing neither for life nor wealth, he went among the dying and the bereaved, 'a guardian angel' to those who escaped the pestilence, 'an angel of mercy' to the families that suffered, raising money for their relief, watching over them and ministering to them ; nor did he fail to point the moral of the visitation, preaching impressively from the words, 'It is better to go to the house of mourning than to the house of feasting.' To one *house of mourning* his thoughts turned with especial tenderness—that which was darkened by the sudden yet peaceful removal of Dr. Adam Clarke, the most illustrious victim of the plague.

Rumours of coming war helped to overshadow the 'dark prospect' of 1832 ; they were discussed in a company where Dawson was present, an honoured, much-admired guest as always. Said one, 'Not such a bad thing if war did break out, after seventeen years of peace; it will clear off the surplus stock of society ; so many needy young sprigs of nobility have shot up and are wanting employment, and there are so many lazy, drunken, profligate ne'er-do-weels among the poor—the scum of all classes will be swept off by the war.'

'An awful way of skimming the pot!' was Dawson's abrupt comment, and it struck silence into him who had spoken too lightly.

But earnestly as he dwelt on these matters, it was only that he might awaken such greater Christian energy as might avert the threatened judgments, by turning the sinners of the land to repentance. No 'croaker' was he, nor could any gloom long overcloud his sunny cheerfulness. Some quaint incidents belong to these very years ; that odd travelling adventure he could tell with such zest, when, his own conveyance breaking down, he and his friends were glad to be taken up into the jolting taxed cart of a farmer, who stood up to drive, despite their civil remonstrances, saying, 'Never mind me! This is how I always stands when I drives *calves*'—all unconscious of what his words implied ; that biting reproof to the well-to-do money-lover, who, with modest reluctance to state how little his charitable givings amounted to, said in broadest Yorkshire, 'What I gives is nought to onybody,' *i. e.*, is nobody's business ; but the reply came promptly, 'Right, fiiend! I believe you do give nothing to anybody.' And it was in 1832 that the famous 'Reform Bill' speech, so daring in its fanciful spiritualising of an unspiritual and contentious subject, was delivered with humorous audacity, in despite of the prudent cautions of the poet-chairman, Montgomery. 'He bowed with great respect to me and to the audience at beginning,' said that gentleman, who had deprecated any political allusion, 'and then took his place in the front of the platform, his broad shoulders so steadily before the chair that I never was able to see the tip of his nose, as if he shunned a rebuking eye because of the line he had taken,' mischievously, and with a visible enjoyment, playing with the fears that he knew would prove groundless ; for sportive as his fancy might be, he always had it well in hand, and was justly sure of himself and of the effects he would produce.

A fresh proof of the 'saving common sense,' which in William Dawson was allied to a poetic imagination, is afforded by his attitude towards a question that was much agitated at this time, when, as is well known, many Christian

minds saw in the threatening evils of the day—the appalling
pestilence, the civil strife and social crime, the imminent
famine and war—signs of the Second Advent of the Lord; and,
giving way to daring speculations, became unbalanced and
unfit for duty. 'You ask my opinion of the Millennium?'
said Dawson to a young relative; 'I really cannot give you
one, as it is a subject that never occupies my attention—

'THIS IS HOW I ALWAYS STANDS WHEN I DRIVES "CALVES."'—*p.* 104.

not knowing any advantage that would accrue to my soul by
studying it. . . . My eyesight is too weak to penetrate the
clouds of prophecy that enshroud it. . . . I shall wait in
God's way, and wait His time, when every cloud will be dis-
persed, and every prophecy fulfilled. "Secret things belong
to God; but the things that are revealed belong to us and
to our children for ever, that we may do all the words of
this law."'

To his sane and steadfast spirit it seemed best to work

for God in the present, instead of trying to read His purposes for the future ; and he was only impelled to greater efforts when the following year deprived the Church of many devoted men ; chief among whom was the grandly-gifted and widely-useful saint of God, Richard Watson. ' Where can we find his equal ? ' he lamented ; but in hope and faith that others would yet follow in the footsteps of the mighty workers gone, he bent himself to do his own part with increased energy, as the demands for his help increased.

Out of twenty-six Sundays only six were often passed at Barwick ; week-day services were frequent at home and abroad. Having returned at midnight from York one day, he had to start for Manchester early next morning. He is at Sheffield this week, at Lynn in Norfolk that week ; he is in London, in Bristol ; and often he is persuaded to stay beyond his allotted time and give services to different places in the same neighbourhood. His iron consti-tution served him well in bearing such fatigues ; and his numerous journeys, being performed chiefly in the open air, did no harm but good to his bodily health. ' Travelled, by cross-roads, in nine days, upwards of two hundred miles, and exercised sixteen times,' is a record of hard, but not hurtful, work ; the cross-road travelling in the breezy country, past woodland and field, repaired the energy that he spent in those strenuous 'exercises.' But few were his journeyings by rail ; it may be doubted if the rattle and rush and weather-fended imprisonment of a train would have braced his nerves as did his outside perch on a coach, or his place in a farmer's gig, or, better, the companionship of a good horse. The active farm-work which filled up every interval of mental or pious toil at home had its own use ; so had the cheerful variety of congenial society into which he was thrown. Despite its arduous character, his was an eminently healthy life ; and often did his full-hearted gratitude break forth when he returned from some 'laborious week' spent in serving man and God. 'Adored be divine Providence for returning me home without the slightest injury ! As was my day, so was my strength. Praise the Lord !'

'Make me a home Christian,' had been his earnest prayer years before, and widely as he wandered he did not neglect his own home and his own people. The society and the chapel at Barwick claimed, and had, very much of his care, even while his colliery agencies multiplied on his hands and caused a great press of business, which he never would either 'mistime or neglect.' An exact and conscientious improvement of every waking hour, a spirit of self-denying industry, enabled him to meet every claim ; and the gentle, pious, helpful niece who managed his household, and repaid by her daughterly care *his* early devotion to mother, sisters, and brothers, found a father's considerate tenderness from him.

This popular favourite had never learnt to prefer his comfort to that of others, and would undergo much inconvenience before he would cause any. He was on a journey and lodged at the house of a friend, who provided for him a bed far too slight to bear his athletic weight ; it gave way as soon as he lay down. But he would disturb no one by asking for better accommodation ; he re-arranged pillows and mattress so as to make a sort of sloping couch from the ruins of the bedstead, and rested as best he could till morning. Again, he arrived, late one cold September evening, at Market Harborough ; the coach set him down at an inn, where he must await another coach which would start at half-past two in the morning. Should he require the weary servants to keep the house open and light and fire burning for him till that hour ? He thought of a way to avoid it. Stepping forth with a cheerful 'Good-night,' he left them to close the doors and retire to rest, under the impression that he was going to stay somewhere in the town ; but he went no farther than one of the stables, where he shared the shelter of the horses till the coach jingled into the yard and he could quietly take his place for home. Not always could he indulge himself in such consideration for others with impunity. Once, being in the Isle of Wight in winter, and coming from a crowded chapel, and much heated too with his exertions, he found prepared for him a bed with 'not a winter but a summer covering. I should,' he owned, 'have asked for more *happing*,' but his strong dislike to giving trouble prevailed, and a severe, and indeed a dangerous, cold was the result. But this was at a later day, when his splendid strength was failing faster than he knew.

It is not necessary to dwell here on the new disturbances which affected Wesleyan Methodism in 1834-35, except as they illustrate anew the character of William Dawson. The agitators, who began with an attack on the 'Theological Institution,' established for the better training of Wesleyan students for the ministry, soon passed on to assail the Wesleyan Constitution at large, and would not desist until the decision of Lord Chancellor Lyndhurst placed that Constitution on a firm and well-defined legal footing. Dawson at first entertained a certain prejudice against the new educational scheme ; but, discerning the real drift of its assailants, he promptly put aside his theoretical objections as of no moment, took the field with a published letter against the contention of Dr. Warren, and sent a subscription of five pounds—large for one of his means—to the funds of the menaced institution. He was too loyal, too modest, too clear-sighted, to hold stiffly by his own opinion on a matter not of vital importance, when such obstinacy would be injurious to the great Christian community to which he belonged, and where he had found such inestimable opportunities of serving his Master.

'I may consider myself in the decline of life,' he remarked to a friend about this time; the bright, piercing eye was beginning to need the aid of glasses, the strong, clear voice was very slightly affected by loss of teeth; 'my grindstones,' said he playfully, 'do not fit each other.' There was, however, rather an increase of activity, and his intellectual faculties seemed stronger as his spiritual life grew brighter. Joyful and contented, whether his outlook was gloomy or promising as to this world, he seemed to gather new power to minister hope and comfort to others when any difficulties beset his own path.

The quaint, striking way in which he would introduce consoling thoughts may be noticed, for it was not only characteristic of the man, but helped much to win acceptance for his counsels. Here, for instance, he is at Colne in a time of great depression and commercial distress. 'We shall have but poor collections,' people whispered. What then? he can give a word of comfort to the desponding. So, before giving out the opening hymn at his first service, he began to tell the people how, as he went preaching from place to place, the various announcements he had been required to make would accumulate in his pockets, until he reached home. They became a useless burden. 'Going into the fields, I take them out, and look at them. I read one— nothing worth keeping in it—I tear it into shreds that the breeze carries off; I look at a second, a third, a fourth— worthless all—I tear them and scatter them in the same way.' With rapid movements of hand and eye he imitated the action of reading, tearing, scattering, and to the eye of fancy the shreds of paper drifted away like snowflakes. The hearers followed his actions and words with wonder; what did this strange introduction mean?

'Now,' said he, 'it is a time of great distress and apprehension with you. Trade is in a bad state, and you are troubled with doubts and fears. Believe me, these fears are worth no more than my useless notes. Throw them to the winds! There is an over-ruling Providence—there is a God and Father who cares for you, His children; trust in Him, and you shall not be confounded,' and with more brave and cheering words he then glided into the hymn:

> 'Give to the winds thy fears;
> Hope and be undismayed:
> God hears thy sighs and counts thy tears,
> God shall lift up thy head;'

which the congregation took up from his lips with enthusiasm answering to his own energy. The sermon that followed breathed courage; and the effect he sought was produced; many who had been full of doubt and dread took new hope, and waited cheerfully for the better times that came.

Another incident relating to this time may be quoted, showing the kindly tact with which he could escape from a difficulty that his own impetuosity had created. He was addressing a missionary meeting gathered in a church of the Particular Baptists; his subject was the favourite one of the 'Sower,' whose 'field is the world.' As with symbolic action he showed the Master scattering His seed, he quoted apposite Scripture passages; and when there leapt to his lips the beloved familiar words, 'He is the propitiation for our sins, and not for ours only, but for the sins of'—he stopped short, turned hesitatingly to the Baptist minister, who sat behind him, and with questioning, eager look, repeated 'of—of—of'; then re-turning towards the congregation, who already were smiling at his hesitation, he added ' of the whole world,' observing, with another half-humorous, apprehensive glance at the pastor, ' It is there ; I cannot help it ; do with it what you like.' Questioned afterwards by a friend as to the motive of his conduct, he said : ' I was full of my subject ; I forgot that I was not, as I am wont to be, in a gathering of my own people ; I had already quoted half that passage, when I remembered where I was, and stopped —but it was too late to go back unperceived. Should I give up my own belief, like a coward ? Should I enter on a defence of it, and so appear as if I designed to insult the good people ? I would do neither, and I am glad the plan I took seemed to give pleasure rather than pain.'

This was but one of several instances where the services of the great Local Preacher were in request for Churches other than his own. Willingly he gave what he could ; but it seemed to some that his increasing toils must be too much for a man who had many secular concerns to attend to. And now once more, and for the last time, it was said, ' Should not this gifted, zealous, successful Evangelist devote *all* his energies to the ministry of the Word ? '

It is the Christmas of the year 1835. There is a meeting gathered at Brunswick Chapel, Leeds, its object to do honour to William Dawson and offer some small acknowledgment of his helpful devotion to the cause of Missions. The Rev. Robert Newton is the chairman ; eloquently he speaks of Mr. Dawson's unremitting exertions for that sacred cause, and is heartily seconded by many other speakers ; and the presentation of Dr. Clarke's *Commentary* to the earnest, eloquent Missionary advocate is well understood as a really ' slight expression ' of the high regard in which his labours are held. Dawson is touched and pleased ; not for praise, not for honour, has he worked ;

and he takes occasion to refer to the great advantages of early consecration, of steady following in the steps of pious parents. It is in connection with the Juvenile Missionary Society that Leeds has most cause to praise him ; he would encourage those young workers, and would not forget how much *he* owes to the teaching of Christian father and mother. Other presentations, from other appreciative friends, are poured in on him ; and in a kind of surprise that the lovers of Missions, in Bradford as in Leeds, should think him worthy of any reward, he says : 'O my Lord ! Thou knowest I am an unprofitable servant. I would render all back to Thee.'

But soon he has to listen to a new plan, by which it is intended to confer on him a more lasting benefit. It is unfolded to him by a Leeds friend, Alderman Scarth, who himself is a chief mover in it.

'We have a scheme on foot,' he is told, 'to raise a fund by subscription, and to settle on you a life income which will set you free from care and toil for a living ; so that you can work for the Church and for Missions without any hindrance. And your brother, who is dependent on you, who would lose his home if he lost you—he shall have a sufficient maintenance secured to him if he outlive you. What do you say ? We hope to raise £200 a year for you. Don't think that anyone dreams that such a sum can ever *reward* you for all your work in the past, or pay for it in the future ! but will you let your Wesleyan friends provide for your comfort, and secure the continuance of your priceless services ? '

William Dawson listened with pleasure and with pain. He feared that he might do wrong if he refused such an offer ; but if he accepted it and the plan were carried out, how much must he give up ! With his farm would go his old home that he loved, his manly independence that he dearly prized.

'It is a hard struggle,' he owned to a friend. . 'This house my father built ; sixty years we have lived in it. My old neighbours, my classes to which I am strongly attached, I must give up these if I give up my farming ; I must no longer be my own master. But I only wish to know the will of God ; then I can make any sacrifice. In which position can I serve God most and honour Him best ? That is the question ! '

He was assured that the sum subscribed—£4,000 was hoped for—should ultimately be devoted to the Missionary cause ; and being persuaded that by a last self-sacrifice he would be of greater use, and would secure the future of his helpless relative, he gave way to the wishes and entreaties of his friends. They were free to make their appeal to the public.

But there was a flaw in the scheme. It was said, ' Let no one subscribe more than one guinea ; thus all Mr. Dawson's friends, rich and poor, may share in the tribute.' We are told, on high authority, that this proviso originated with Dawson himself. It is consonant with what we know of his independent character that he should prefer to benefit by a genuinely popular subscription rather than by the gifts of a few rich men. But this feeling, so natural in him, was not to be gratified in the way he might have wished. The restriction had to be withdrawn, the Missionary Committee had to take the matter in hand, before a proper provision for the great preacher could be realised. A year and a half passed in rather trying uncertainty ; he could neither manage his farm to advantage, nor give legal notice to quit. Yet faithfully and patiently he worked and waited, though he was sometimes troubled at the thought that his difficult sacrifice might have been made in vain. ' It was the benefit to the Missionary cause that conquered my will,' said he; and he shrank from any suggestion that Missionary funds should be taxed for his support, that the deficient subscriptions should be made up from Missionary collections. Nor did he like it when a friend said jestingly:

'You may have to *sit down* with £100 a year.'

'Nay, it is not for *sitting down* that I should have it, but for *rising up*,' was his quick reply. More work, not less, was what he designed to do. During this time of suspense he rather increased his exertions; his extra journeys in one twelvemonth reached a hundred; eight days saw him in six places remote from each other, holding thirteen services and covering 432 miles by the help of the 'heavy coaches,' on which he was an outside passenger, often in 'tremendous wet weather.' Yet he would return home with an air of such refreshment as if he had taken a pleasant morning walk, and, apparently unfatigued, would at once betake himself to the task next at hand—whether it was answering the accumulated letters from many different quarters which commonly awaited him, or setting off to fulfil some pious duty connected with his classes or his charities, or negotiating for ground whereon a new chapel might be raised in a neighbouring village. Barwick had to thank his efforts for the Sunday-school which was opened there; and now Saxton was indebted to his influence with the Gascoigne family for a proper site for the much-needed place of worship.

Those who enjoyed his society saw no abatement in its lively attractiveness during this time of uncertainty, no trace of pre-occupation with his own concerns. His talk sparkled with its old lustre when he dwelt on 'fictitious' religious feeling. 'It is easy to detect,' he said; 'God's fingers when they touch the soul, leave it shining—man's fingers leave a stain; the soul is really blacker for the clumsy attempt to imitate the work of the Spirit. As well try to imitate the sun in the firmament!' And dwelling joyously on the heroes of faith who had 'run in the race of eternal life,' and on the growing splendour of the prize that appeared far off to Abraham, a glimpse of the day of Christ, but had become to Paul 'an eternal weight of glory,' to John 'likeness' to the Lord Himself, he said gladly, 'In an earthly race, men tire; here, they renew their strength.'

It was the secret of his own unwearied effort under every difficulty.

He was setting off on a preaching tour to the north when the decisive letter from the Secretary of the Missionary Committee was put into his hand. 'Father, Thy will be done!' he said when he had read it. His perplexities were solved, his doubts were past. He should have much of the freedom he loved; for half the year he should preach where he would, to whom he would; only six months out of twelve should be devoted wholly to the Mission cause, 'not continuously, but as the interests of the Missionary Society shall appear to require.'

The proposal at first made, that *all* or nearly all his time should be given to that one object, had always repelled him. 'I could not do it,' he had said when laying his case before the Committee by letter, after the matter had been duly discussed in the Conference of 1837; 'I have neither mental variety nor yet physical energy for the employment; I must, therefore, shrink from the task.' His plea was accepted; the promptings of the kind heart that made him anxious to serve all his brethren who might need him were respected. An income that he deemed sufficient was to be secured to him, and a provision for his brother. He accepted all with serious, cheerful thankfulness. What though the moderate anticipations of his friends had not been fulfilled, and his means would be more straitened than they had meant? still the yearly £150 might supply all his needs. 'Let me live to glorify my God, to publish the Gospel—what matters all besides?' was his steadfast thought.

And now our 'Yorkshire farmer' must leave his farm-stead at Barnbow, his well-loved fields and flocks, and in his sixty-fifth year he becomes a town-dweller, taking a modest house in 'Springfield Terrace, Burmantofts, Leeds,' where Mary Dawson, his loving, sensible, pious niece, continues her care for his comfort, and that of his brother. Did he miss the pleasant outlook from the house his father had built, over the fields and meadows he himself had tilled so long—and the singing of the larks that soared over all and rejoiced his poetic heart? He did undoubtedly feel 'the sacrifice of all his associations, connected with all the pleasures he had enjoyed in that obscure place, scarcely known in the world—Barnbow,' but so seldom was he at home in his own 'hired house' that there was little leisure for indulging in any regrets, even had he been one who was prone to such indulgence. Happily, it was his principle and practice to look backwards with thankfulness and forwards with hope ; and it appeared as if the step he had taken, with some small misgiving, was to be fully justified by the results; so wide a prospect of usefulness seemed opening to him. The demands for his services came thick and threefold, now that his admirers supposed him free to comply with them all. It became necessary for an official plan of his *missionary* engagements to be drawn up, and he himself made careful arrangements to meet all claims upon him that could be met ; but did he go wherever he was called, he must compress two years' work into one.

'Uncle,' said Mary Dawson at last, 'your labour is too oppressive. You should contrive, in arranging your work, to secure two or three days now and then for rest.'

'Mary,' he replied, ' I shall *rest* in my grave. The night cometh when no man can work.'

He broke fresh ground when, in the autumn of 1838, he went into Wales to address the English-speaking inhabitants of many places in the south of the Principality ; Carmarthen saw him and heard him, Tenby and Haverfordwest, Milford Haven and Swansea. He noted with an eager intelligence all that was new and striking in the ways of the unfamiliar country, as he and his companions traversed it by mountainous road and sluggish coach and storm-tossed ferry-boat; the beauty of the scenery was what least interested him ; his eye, as he often lamented, had not been properly trained to appreciate the picturesque in nature or in art ; but to every point of human interest he was awake and alive. The musical speech of the people struck him, the simplicity and contentment of the peasantry, who fed cheerfully on barley-bread, and went about stockingless and shoeless very often ; the little lowly churches, the snow-white lime-washed cottages, the graveyards, where the curiously decorated graves 'appeared like white-painted coffins, filled with earth and set with flowers,' drew his attention by the sharp contrast they offered to the scenes he knew best ; especially was he struck by the 'simple, artless, honest' faces of the Welsh maidens, glowing with health under their broad-brimmed steeple-hats ; he thought sadly of the sallow cheeks and stunted shapes of the poor factory-girls in his own Yorkshire, who are still suffering from their cruelly long hours, not yet shortened by law. Hundreds of these bright-faced Welsh girls are gathered together for hiring as servants at 'St. Clear's,' where the missionary speakers have to change coach; it is said that four pounds a year is the highest wage they can look for. Are the more highly-paid town-dwellers as well off?

Such thoughts mingled irresistibly with diviner musings, while Dawson passed along the rough Welsh roads of that day, rejoicing in the kindly welcome he met everywhere, and in the numerous signs of good effected in this land where he found himself 'a sort of foreigner.'

Very shortly after this Welsh tour was ended, the Evangelist was engaged in a journey by sea and land to London, and to Maidstone, Ramsgate, Margate, Chelsea, and Dover—troublesome, but willingly taken to oblige various friends who begged for his help. Thus it was not till the close of the year that he could take his share in the exciting scenes connected with the celebration of the 'Centenary of Wesleyan Methodism.' Speaking in December at the adjourned meeting held in Brunswick Chapel, Leeds, he dwelt with joy on the brotherly unity of feeling and purpose which now bound together all within those walls —a happy contrast with recent troublous scenes— and then gave a quaint, true description of his own career.

'I was always a nondescript,' said he, 'an itinerant local preacher—a sort of link between the travelling and local preachers—something like the Acts of the Apostles between the Gospels and the Epistles, uniting the two. A friend of mine said once, "When Matthew Henry died, he was in the Acts of the Apostles." "That," said I, "is where I would be when I die—in the Acts of the Apostles."' And he had his wish. Apostolic in his zeal, he only gave up his apostolic toils with his life.

'I exercised a *sort of preachment*,' he went on, 'some years before I became a decided Methodist, but I found it would not do to be halting between the Established Church and the Methodists, and gave myself to the latter, soul and body—head, heart, and hand.' It is possible that in dwelling on this whole-souled devotion, which was the only merit he claimed for himself, he had some thought of those whom he ranked as 'skin-deep Methodists,' easily drawn aside by attractions other than spiritual to leave the communion he loved. Their example he deprecated, and would fain never see it followed more.

The early part of 1839 was fully occupied with engagements already contracted, distinguished only by the success that now seemed always to attend the efforts of the widely-known preacher. As of yore, chapels often proved too small for the congregations that gathered to hear him, and he would be compelled to preach in the open air, perhaps in the close neighbourhood of a stack-yard, itself thronged with young and old, who found perches on walls and carts and stacks, whence they could see and hear the speaker round whom a dense mass of hearers clustered, hanging in breathless attention on his lips while he spoke of that possession common to all, 'a jewel called the soul—divine in its origin, astonishing in its properties, and, though fallen from its glory, inestimable in its value,' and denounced 'the indescribable, inexpressible, inconceivable folly of the man that barters away this jewel, get what he will in exchange.' It was natural and easy for him, who willingly gave his all to the service of his fellow-creatures, to urge on them not only the wisdom but the joy of a like consecration of life, strength, and means to the grand work of arousing men to see the value of this mysterious possession, of persuading them not for any price the world could give to cheat themselves out of an eternity of growing glory and bliss—to plead how there was no pleasure so great, no duty so binding on Christian men, as the pleasure and the duty of

soul-saving. The response to his plea was immediate and
great, not only in contributions to the missionary cause
which he sought to serve, but in the quickened sense of duty
and privilege that outlasted the occasion. It was the latter
result which he most prized; the ample sums which men
would give under the compelling power of his eloquence
pleased him indeed, but his pleasure was much dashed if he
saw no clear evidence of the spiritual benefit that he yearned
to confer. Was it not possible, he asked sometimes appre-
hensively, that the 'collection,' following the sermon, dissi-
pated thought and deadened conviction? But it hardly
suited him better when, on some few occasions, an
entrance-fee admitted privileged hearers to 'reserved seats'
in places of worship where he ministered; it was 'present-
ing so many silver daggers' at the people who came to
hear what should be a free Gospel; and perforce he had to
remain content with the ordinary way of proceeding, as a
lesser evil.

Rapidly, amid a constant succession of services like the
one described, the year ran on until July, when he began
his six months' round of work under the orders of the Missionary Committee. It was sufficiently arduous, covering
very much of the Midlands and not a little of the south
of England, and often requiring him to preach twice a day,
and to attend missionary meetings also. In one month
twenty-five sermons and fifteen addresses were delivered
while travelling 886 miles—almost always, we must remember, without help of steam, and sometimes in open
conveyances, while 'the rains descended and the floods
came,' overwhelming the hopeful harvest of the farmer and
imperilling his cattle. Passing through such scenes of distress, William Dawson thought and said nothing of his own
bodily discomfort, all his anxiety being for the agriculturist,

and for the general misery that might result ; it was something of a pity, certainly, that lanes, 'knee-deep in water,' prevented many persons from attending public worship, while others were perforce engaged in rescuing their drowning beasts from the flood ; but no personal feeling intruded itself for a moment.

The selflessness—if we may borrow a new-coined word—-that shone out in circumstances which, like these, might have annoyed some men, intent on their own successes and pleasures, was evident also in the candid simplicity with which Dawson would refer to certain deficiencies in his own powers or their development. Returning from a six weeks' tour that had taken him through Windsor, he spoke with delight of the royal castle, of its 'antiquity, grandeur, and majesty,' adding that he had seen in many of its rooms paintings that he supposed to be excellent—something in the colouring and the grouping pleased him ; but he knew not why. 'I was grieved at myself,' he said ; he felt that his pleasure was ignorant and might be ill-founded. 'If I have *any* taste, it belongs more immediately to the ear than to the eye,' he confessed ; and even in music, which delighted him, he would not have claimed to take anything but uninstructed pleasure. There are those who would more willingly own to grave wrong-doing than to such defects in perception ; but in Dawson's large composition there was no room for the small miseries of vanity and false shame. The work on which he was heart and soul intent was too great.

To the moral picturesque our Yorkshire farmer was always keenly alive ; and with the eye of an accomplished critic he judged the lights and shades of the new scenes that opened on him when, in his sixty-seventh year, he crossed the sea to make his first visit to Ireland, taking that country also into his missionary journeyings. Ireland before the Famine stands vividly pictured in his correspondence—the Ireland of Father Mathew, whom the English visitor sees at his much-needed work, 'going through the land lecturing on the teetotal system, and obtaining pledges to adopt it.' He is in Dublin when Dawson reaches it; and we may, if we like, take our stand beside the two men, on the steps of a public building, besieged by some three thousand persons; a wall of defence between the speaker and the crowd is made by some scores of police and a few mounted soldiers, who keep a clear space in front of the steps, while Mathew, the interesting-looking man in middle life, speaks briefly, 'not very fluently,' but earnestly, on the blessings of temperance. The surging masses of the people —ragged, dirty, poverty-stricken—listen as to an angel of God; and, the address being over, they stream forward in their hundreds, fall on their knees upon the dirty steps at his feet, fix eyes of unutterable earnestness on him as he speaks, and with great devotion echo the words of the pledge as he repeats it; then retiring, they make way for another human wave to flow forward in their place. And now Dawson and the friend who has brought him would withdraw; the police open the way from the retiring crowd, but it is not easy to pass through the throngs of women, some pitiably diseased, some clasping sickly infants in their arms, all trying to get near the Father, and entreating that he will heal the sick—they think he can do it with a touch. He does not appear to enjoy it; he keeps his hands behind him. Indeed, this mistaken, half-idolatrous homage was very painful to its object. 'But I think,' says Dawson, 'he should have retired from their presence, and have said to those who fell on their knees before him, as Peter did to Cornelius, "Stand up; I myself also am a man." Oh, that one could have preached the pure Gospel to them, and secured thousands of heart-pledges for Jesus Christ! but there was no allusion to the need of pardon for the past, a new heart, a new spirit, through faith in the blood of the Lamb. This is a very serious defect,' he adds, with true insight, as though he had foreseen how not a few of these temperance pledges, taken with such touching earnestness,

HE WATCHED THE POOR PEASANTS AT THEIR MAKESHIFT AGRICULTURE.—*p.* 124.

would be broken or evaded—kept in the letter, broken in the spirit—when the wild excitement of the hour was gone. Knowing the terrible strength of the 'Devil's chain' of drunkenness, he feared lest these poor slaves of habit, who were looking to man and not to God for deliverance, would not long remain free from their bondage.

Help they sorely needed, and his heart yearned over them in their misery. Passing through the country he saw the wretched homes whence those thousands had poured to kneel at the feet of Mathew—cabins walled with mud mixed with straw, windowless, chimneyless, the smoke oozing through the thatch or pouring from the open doorway; hovels a shade less wretched, since they boasted a chimney, advertising ' very good beds for travellers.'   He noted within some fifty English miles, 'more spirit shops in the villages than we have beer-shops in England,' every poor alehouse sold spirits, so did almost every grocer.   With a farmer's eye he watched the poor peasants at their makeshift agriculture.   'They get a little land and cultivate it by the spade, set their potatoes, and the rest of their time is not half employed.'   As for those who could not obtain their acre or two, and a few potatoes to plant, their huts were in a state that the English poor would find incredible.   In the open streets of the little market towns sat many busy cobblers, mending for the folk who came long distances to market their much-worn shoes, 'many of which, with us, would be thrown on the dunghill'; why was such pathetic effort at economy needed ?   One reason was apparent in the swarming spirit-shops; another in the lack, throughout the southern districts, of any industry but inefficient agriculture.   'There is more than twice the number of people to cultivate the land than is necessary.'   But was this all ?

There were bright patches of light amidst this gloom. Warm and glowing was the cordial Irish welcome that greeted the visitors everywhere; blessing seemed to follow their words; there was much worth, piety, zeal, among the ' few Methodists of the south of Ireland,' whom Dawson rejoiced to serve, and whose appearance bore witness to wholesome, industrious, useful lives, while in their well-appointed homes the Missionary advocates were 'treated like priests and kings.'   All the more he mourned over the debased condition of their Romanist countrymen, sunk in superstition, and steeped in poverty that seemed hopeless, their chief solace and their chief snare the destructive habit of dram-drinking. It would be well if 'the commanding influence of the priests' could reach and check that one vice. But what had that mighty ascendency of the priesthood accomplished for the richly-gifted race of men who had so long bowed to its sway, and now sat in apathetic misery at its feet?

For the first time William Dawson was addressing scanty congregations, to be counted in scores of decent, well-doing people, while all around were thousands of half-starved suffering creatures, their souls perishing for lack of knowledge; yet his voice could not reach them—they would not hear it.

'Oh, to preach the pure Gospel to them!'

CHAPTER IX.

THE LAST YEARS OF SERVICE.

SOME sad forebodings clouded William Dawson's thoughts when he left the Green Isle, over which the shadow of impending calamity seemed to brood. He was not to see the years of famine and pestilence that were near at hand, nor the following period of European revolution and upheaval; but in the actual state of things there was much which filled him with apprehension of an approaching crisis, 'when opposing elements, religious and political, would ignite and burst into ruinous conflagration.' He was distressed by the fraud and dishonesty that in the commercial world were producing widespread disaster and suffering; he mourned over those who, 'making haste to be rich,' had pierced themselves with many sorrows; nor could he be blind to the spread of strange opinions which seemed to him unscriptural, uncharitable, and fraught with danger in the religious world; to the threatenings of discontent among the people of the land, who were seeking wild remedies for their poverty and misery. But, said he, 'Our nation has often been in an awful state, and the Lord has undertaken for us and delivered us; He reigns, as Head over all things, to His body the Church'; and cheering himself with this thought, he eagerly resumed his busy toil among his own countrymen. We may trace him here and there through the year; now he is preaching on the death of a beloved and most useful friend and follower, the father of David Stoner; now he is describing himself as 'a poor man, four days out of employment,' and anxious to obtain it ; then he is opening chapels in one place, delivering missionary addresses in another. If there is monotony in the story there was none in the style of the speaker.

We may still see and hear him as he was at this time, for the eloquent pen of Dr. Gregory has described how he looked and spoke on the occasion of a memorable missionary meeting at Pontefract, where the Leeds District Committee was gathered. Dawson had doffed his farmer's garb—being now entirely set apart to the work of the Lord —and put on the ministerial black. And the change became him admirably. On the platform he drew himself up and seemed some inches taller than he really was. He was big-boned, sinewy, stalwart, farmer-limbed, and farmer-faced. His light-grey eyes became almost fiercely incandescent as he kindled with his theme. 'His face was embrowned by outdoor toil and travel.' The speech he gave on this occasion was 'the most famous and effective of all Dawson's platform deliverances—his *telescopic* speech. Coiling up his resolution into the shape of a spy-glass, he described in the most animated, energetic, vivid style, characteristic scenes of existing heathenism, asking before each description, "What do I see ?" Then, turning in another direction, he demanded, " But what do I see in the distant prospect ?" He then depicted the most graphic scenes of millennial peace and love and glory. Of course his real telescope for "the distant prospect" was the mighty tube of prophecy. It was a great privilege to hear William Dawson at the very top of his oratorical powers. A famous London barrister, himself a powerful and popular speaker, said in my hearing, "I have heard all, or nearly all, the greatest orators of my time, but I never heard such overwhelming eloquence as that of William Dawson when he turned his resolution into a spy-glass, and described the present and the future of missionary enterprise. I have dwelt the more on this," says the witness, so admirably qualified to judge in the matter of sacred eloquence, " because, strange to say, his biographer, whilst doing the fullest justice to Dawson in the pulpit, passes over his at least equal power on the platform. We there saw both his physique and his intellectual stature at full length." '

This vivid description, which shows with what freshness Dawson could invest an address already celebrated, makes manifest also with what unabated, glowing confidence he looked past the cloud and darkness of the present to the future glories of Christ's Kingdom in this world. Priceless was that gift of inspired imagination ! He knew well its value in another, and would not have it repressed ; and in his own quaint way he took the part of that young preacher of splendid promise, whose appreciative words we have just quoted, and who, he found, had been much too sharply checked for the ' juvenile efflorescence' of a sermon, rich in fancy and feeling, preached under circumstances of singular difficulty, before this very District Meeting.

' So I hear,' said Dawson to the two grave critics who had distinguished themselves by severity, 'you have been falling foul of that imaginative young fellow. Ah, well, pare him down, and by the time he is as old as you are, he'll be about as dry as you are.'

William Dawson did not stand alone in outspoken sympathy for the roughly handled probationer of genius ; but no one else would have expressed the feeling with such homely significant audacity. Happily the *paring-down* process he deprecated was not pushed further, and the consequent loss to Methodism, its pulpit, pastorate, and literature, did not ensue.

No one who at this time looked on the farmer-evangelist

in his manly strength, and listened to his impassioned eloquence, could have imagined that he was, as he said, 'on the decline'; but he had good reason for that opinion as respected his bodily health, and some warm friends of his persuaded him, with difficulty, to undergo a medical examination. 'There is water on the chest,' pronounced the doctor who was called in. 'My mother died of that complaint,' said the patient very calmly; he listened with mild composure to the warning that, if he did not relax in his public exertions, the consequences might be very serious, but he did not see his way to obeying; he had engagements to fulfil that seemed imperative, and his earnest desire to 'work while it was day' was still paramount. Amid incessant toil the year ran on to its close, when we find him in York. There, at the Missionary Meeting, he delivered his famous 'Railway Speech,' so startling in its spiritualising of an unspiritual subject; and so doing he drew on himself the censure of such a critic as he had once compared to 'a horse-fly, choosing the sore part of a horse's back to revel on, to the neglect of the sound unbroken flesh.'

The newspaper oracle admitted that 'the speaker's meaning was good, that the speech produced a good impression,' but could not away with the errors of taste involved in such eccentricities of illustration. The lofty condemnation included Dawson's hearers as well as himself. A better judge on such matters, having remarked that 'Mr. Dawson was in every respect a man *sui generis*, and must not be tried by the rules that applied to other speakers,' added that, 'though the taste of some of his most splendid coruscations might be questioned, their power over a certain class of minds was irresistible,' and in its remarkable success, in the lasting good produced, may be found the sufficient justification of a style that '*could* not be imitated.'

Dawson, we know, was well content to be esteemed illiterate and unpolished, if he could benefit the multitudes who did not understand learned and polite eloquence. He was not troubled by the fastidious fault-finder who now attacked him ; other thoughts were paramount. 'Farewell, John,' he said to a young friend in this December, 'this is perhaps the last time I shall see you on earth. I have a presentiment that I shall go off suddenly, and you must not be surprised if you hear of me being found dead some-where ;' and with such a feeling strong in his mind he hastened on to fulfil the pledge he had given to friends in the Isle of Wight and London. 'The night cometh when no man can work' was ever in his thoughts.

From that journey he returned with difficulty ; the severe cold brought on by his comfortless lodging at one place was aggravated into pleurisy by his attempt to dis-regard his sufferings and continue his work. He reached home only just in time. Sharp and prompt medical treat-ment checked the malady, but the friendly doctor forbade all exertion for a fortnight at least. He was surrounded by faithful affection, he was tended with the most loving care ; and thankful for these comforts, and for 'the best of all, sweet heart-cheering tokens of the Divine presence,' he sub-mitted patiently to that which was 'quite a new cross—being shut out of pulpit-work and shut up in the parlour.'

Yet it was a heavy cross. 'My Master, Jesus, is so excellent, that I always feel my soul in its element when engaged in His service,' he wrote from his sick-room. 'When actively employed in His work, I seem to move round Him as my centre, and find most delightful rest when I am in my orbit, moving in my circle. I would still move on without cessation in that orbit.' Assured of having all eternity to rest in, he was, perhaps, too ready to believe himself sufficiently restored, and to resume the labours that he loved. He looked out from his enforced seclusion with wistful eye at the threatening evils, moral and social and spiritual, that surrounded him; they troubled him more than his own pain or weariness ever could, and he longed to be up and doing again—doing battle against the forces of sin, and for his Master.

With amended health, he entered on the duties of the year 1841; but he soon was made aware that it was not with him as it had been in days gone by; his splendid strength was giving way fast. Not so his mental energy. Visiting Nottingham, he surprised his hearers with a richly imaginative discourse on the Church of Christ, personified as 'the King's daughter, all glorious within, her clothing of wrought gold,' with 'raiment of needlework.' With his usual ingenuity, he caught the attention of his hearers by imagery borrowed from the beautiful art-industries of Nottingham—its 'lace-work and needle-work,' but lingered not long on these, 'making everything tell on the conscience and understanding,' so that the sermon, connected with a very extraordinary spiritual influence on the people, became extensively useful.

'No, it is not altogether new,' said the preacher to a friend. 'I took it once at Manchester, in Oldham Street Chapel, on the evening of Dr. Warren's return from his Chancery trial in London, when the Society was balancing, and when it was unknown a short time before, whether or no I should be allowed to occupy the pulpit. Since then I have had her, in true Oriental style, though the daughter of a king, locked up, and have not once suffered her to go abroad till to-night.' Those who listened to this discourse found the 'King's daughter' glorious indeed. The *beauty of holiness* that is her rightful bridal clothing was set

forth in such attractive colours as to win every heart.   But of
this only twice-delivered sermon no adequate report remains.

Ere long William Dawson was in Lincolnshire, preaching occasional sermons with his wonted fire and fervour,
but with unwonted difficulty to himself ; and now at last he
confessed to a friendly ear that he was unequal to his task.
' I shall go on till July,' he said, 'and then I shall state
to the Committee that I must become a supernumerary.'

Could he have brought himself to speak as openly to
the Committee as to his friend, his labours would at once
have been lightened and his health might have benefited.
But to him such a step seemed a breach of good faith.   Not
only his keen delight in his work, but his sense that it was
' a debt ' which he owed to the Church, forbade him to
desist while it seemed humanly possible for him to fulfil the
obligations he held sacred.

In the March of 1841, the home of his married brother
Richard, at Acaster, received him for three days—a longer
time than he had spent with his own kinsfolk during many
years.   It was a little family festival, for they celebrated his
birthday ; he was now sixty-eight.   Well and deservedly he
was beloved in that home, where the good old farmer-life
of Barnbow was continued; and its sons and daughters were
loved by him with a father's love.   But the joy of the
reunion was a little overcast by the evident feebleness and
suffering of the guest.   The difficult breathing and the
cough which had long troubled him were visibly worse.
His sister-in-law said some words of tender warning to him,
and he answered composedly, ' I believe I am suffering
from the complaint of which my mother died,' but his
sunny cheerfulness and steady courage were not therefore
impaired.   To him there was no terror in the thought of
' sudden death '

'What is it but crossing the River of Death where it is narrowest, and being wafted over the stream in a few minutes?'

So he had spoken when another faithful servant of his Master was called away to receive his reward at a few moments' notice; he had said of *William Bramwell* that he was 'unusually favoured' in the fashion of his removal from this world—no lingering sickness, no long delaying on the stormy shore of that cold river; and the summons he did not fear to meet was to come to William Dawson in like manner, as he would have desired. 'The pins of my tabernacle *must* loosen, and the canvas must have its rents and holes. The leading wish of my heart is, as expressed in the hymn which I often say and sing,—

> ' Let me in life, in death,
>   Thy steadfast truth declare,
> And publish with my latest breath,
>   Thy love and guardian care.'

These touching words, which occur in a letter addressed to an anxious friend about this time, sufficiently describe the habitual feeling of their writer's mind, while, with no doubtful consciousness of peril to life and health, he went about the work of his appointed Missionary tour which began in April, and which was to take in, as before, many places in the Midlands, and some few north, west, and south.

He can be traced at Dover and at Canterbury: his discerning host Mr. Geden, noted well the impressive power of his ministry at both places, the spirituality of his conversation, and the pathetic fervour of his address to the son of the house, then just entering on that ministerial career of distinguished usefulness which has not long been closed. As if he were bestowing a farewell blessing, Dawson laid his hand on the young man's head, and said:

'Live when I am dead—live better than I have lived!' words in which the presentiment of approaching departure is quite visible.

The latter part of June found him in London, at Tunbridge Wells, at Croydon, taking an active part in various public services, and neither speaking nor looking like one whose courage was chilled by the 'shadow of death.' 'No Christian need fear a shadow!' he had once said with healthy scorn.

His last sermons were preached at Great Berkhampstead in the St. Albans Circuit; for finding he had some days free for extra work, he had given these to the friends who were opening a new chapel in that tranquil Hertfordshire village, honoured as the birthplace of William Cowper. A large congregation, gathered from many surrounding places, listened to Dawson on the evening of the 1st of July, while he dwelt on the text, 'And now the ax is laid to the root of the tree; therefore every tree which bringeth not forth good fruit is hewn down and cast into the fire.' He spoke as a good husbandman, who knew well how fruit-bearing trees must be dealt with, and gave many a homely striking illustration of those solemn words of the Baptist, whose sternly faithful warnings he enforced with all his old vigour. Then, referring to the doctrine of divine Providence, he spoke with earnest thankfulness of the guiding Hand that had directed his own doings and had protected him and his family.

'I can "set to my seal that God is true" as it respects the faithfulness of our promise-making, promise-keeping God, in the fulfilment of His word to a fatherless family. In my own experience, and those of my brothers and sisters, I can bear witness to this truth—that as it regards the word spoken to the widow and the fatherless—"faithful is He that hath promised, who also will do it." I can lift up my voice, and say, "Blessed be the Lord who gave us rest according to all that He hath promised; there hath not failed one word of all His good promise that He promised," by His servants who wrote as they were "moved by the Holy Ghost."'

Such, and yet more fervent, were the words of heart-cheering gratitude which Dawson addressed to the congregation who heard his last pulpit utterances.

His friends recalled afterwards how he had said of this particular text : 'I never feel my mind impressed to preach upon it, but it is almost invariably followed by a sudden death.'

From Hertfordshire he came direct to Leeds ; and alighting from the train, he was going to take a cab for himself and his luggage. But a noisy dispute now arose between two cabmen as to the right of conveying him, and growing weary of their wrangling, Mr. Dawson dismissed them both with a flash of humorous vexation ; he would carry his portmanteau himself.

How lightly the 'Yorkshire farmer' would have borne such a load in days gone by ! but now it was too much for him. Breathless and panting, he must stop at a friend's door, and leave his burden there, while he made his slow way home.

Here was another warning; but when refreshed by a few hours' rest, he felt all himself again, and answered various pressing letters, making plans for further exertions ; then he betook himself to a friend's house, where with a numerous party he watched the quaint ceremony of 'chairing' the newly elected members of Parliament ; he had not lost any of his interest in public matters. But some one saying, 'You do not look well,' he said, significantly

touching his breast, 'Not right here,—my work is too hard
for me,' he added, half reluctantly.   People urged on him
to see a doctor, to stay at home awhile ; a minister present
offered to take his next appointment, if he would but   .
consent to rest.

'No ; I am never so well as in the open air, and
travelling.   I trust the journey I have to take will do me
good and not harm,' he replied.   As he returned on foot to
his own house, however, his kinswoman, Mrs. Phillips, who
accompanied him, saw with alarm how the small exertion
overtaxed him ; and again he was entreated to call in a
medical man : to take a few days' rest.

'My journey to-morrow will be the best medicine I can
take,' he replied with cheerful persistence ; he thought that
all his experience warranted this opinion.   Fresh air and
movement had always been his grand panacea.   So, on the
morning of the 3rd of July he set off to Colne in Lancashire to keep his engagement with the friends there, his
relative, Mr. Phillips, accompanying him, and staying with
him at the house of another member of that family.

He was surrounded with affectionate friends, watchful
over his health.   Cheerfully as ever he greeted them, and
happily he spent the evening hours among them, choosing
the tunes that he wished to have sung in the chapel on the
following day, joining in singing several hymns, and closing
the day with earnest prayer to which all listened, well
pleased that his fervent utterance seemed to show no abatement of strength.   But there was some sign of past suffering
in his looks.   'He may be better now, but he has been
unwell—he should have a light burning in his room all
night,' some one said ; and his travelling companion would
fain have persuaded him to allow himself this small luxury.

'O child, I am much better—there is no need of it—

blow it out,' he replied, with a cheery unwillingness to be treated as an invalid ; and he was left to his quiet rest.

But in the gray twilight of the summer morning Mr. Phillips woke suddenly ; a faint voice was in his ear, 'Edward, get up—I am very poorly,' and springing up he saw that Mr. Dawson had risen, and stood there struggling for breath. To help him to a chair, to alarm the family, to send for a doctor, was the work of a few minutes. But little could be done. The attempt to open a vein and give some relief to the labouring chest proved futile.

Leaning back in his chair, and feebly grasping his staff, William Dawson spoke a few farewell words to the loving friends who hung over him in distress—precious words, that showed how calm, clear, and bright burnt the flame of his spirit's life, of his Christian hope.

> 'Let us in life, in death,
>   Thy steadfast truth declare,'

were the last syllables he could frame clearly. Trying to add the concluding lines of the verse—

> 'And publish with our latest breath
>   Thy love and guardian care,'

utterance failed him. He crossed his hands over his breast, and without a struggle, without one lingering groan, 'ceased at once to work and live.'

Happy was William Dawson in his life; his cheerful, un-wearied activity in his Master's cause had the reward he most coveted, for many were the sinners who by his words were turned from darkness to light, from the power of Satan to God.

Happy was he in his death ; no slowly wasting malady shut him out from his loved employment and made life a heavy burden ; not for a day did he outlive his usefulness.

When the first sharp touch of pain warned him that his day's work might soon be done, his mind rested calmly on the promise, ' Fear not, I am with thee ; be not dismayed, I am thy God' ; and the faithful human friends who were about him at the last saw with mingled grief and joy how the promise was fulfilled ; how the Presence kept him from all fear or shrinking as, at 'the narrowest place,' he forded the shadowy river.

There was wide-spread grief when the news of that sudden departure spread abroad, and first the people in Colne, and then the thousands who had cause to bless the hour they saw the face of William Dawson, made haste to do honour to his memory. Very early on the Monday morning his sorrowing friends prepared to remove his remains to his own home ; but crowds were already astir, who reverently escorted the hearse on its way, singing the hymns he had loved, and other crowds met the mournful train at every town through which it passed towards Leeds, showing the same deep feeling. Again and again the verse was chanted which he had tried to repeat in his last moments, and which well summed up his life's work.

Two days later his funeral procession passed through Leeds on its way to Barwick, where his kinsfolk wished to lay him beside his mother in the old churchyard ; and the streets and high-roads by which they went were packed and lined with masses of sympathising spectators, heedless of the heavy rain that fell on them and on the long lines of mourners who went before and followed after the hearse, on foot, on horseback, in carriages. There was a general anxiety on the part of the townsfolk to show all esteem for the single-hearted evangelist who had loved the souls of his fellow-creatures better than his own life ; but the most touching spectacle was witnessed at Barwick. Here had been

William Dawson's home, in that farmstead which from the brow of a hill looked down on the dark array of mourners, as they passed with songs of joy and sadness; here he was known best and prized the most. Sorrowing friends of all ranks joined the funeral company, filled and overflowed the church, and stood weeping round the grave, while the solemn voice of the Rector pronounced:

' " I heard a voice from heaven, saying unto me, Write, from henceforth blessed are the dead which die in the Lord; even so, saith the Spirit: for they rest from their labours." '

'And their works follow them !' many a heart that heard would have responded. Here, where almost all his years had passed, there were few indeed who had not loved the departed in life, and on whom his ministry had not conferred benefits that would last for ever.

No tribute of grateful affection that Methodists could bestow was withheld from him who had freely given himself to Methodism, 'body and soul—heart, head, and hand.' Memorial services were held, eloquent sermons were preached in his honour, biographies written and eagerly welcomed; but perhaps nothing would so well have pleased him as the contributions to the Mission cause which many of his friends gave as the fittest thankoffering to God who had raised up William Dawson as an advocate for Missions.

Far beyond his own time his power has been felt for good; so long, so lovingly has he been remembered by those who once knew and heard him; such delight have they taken in reproducing for a younger generation his quaint impressive words, his startling warnings, his irresistible appeals—so vividly have they set the very man before us — that perhaps of no great preacher of his time could it have been so truly said, 'He being dead, yet speaketh.'

The reasons of this fond and faithful remembrance must not be sought only in the essentially popular character of Dawson's original genius, in that pictorial imagination and those flashes of irresistible humour and pathos which had lent to his oratory much of the varied charm of a dramatic representation, but also in the rich humanity of the great preacher, who had been so pre-eminently 'one who loved his fellow-men,' who delighted in their society, and delighted yet more in serving them. He was unwearied in doing kindnesses, and thought himself well repaid by the success of his well-meant efforts, and there was something very endearing in the homeliness of speech and the unpretending simplicity of character which in him were united to excellent, manly common sense and unselfish devotion. That, all his life long, he was a man of many warm and faithful friendships, that he watched with anxious, tender care over the young relatives on whom his strong domestic affections expended themselves, is evident in his correspondence ; we may draw attention in particular to a series of letters, remarkable for their kindly, practical wisdom, their judicious counsels, addressed to the nephew whom, with wistful delight, he saw preparing to give himself to the great work of the ministry. The heart of love in him did not thus satisfy itself; it overflowed, as we have seen, to all who were desolate and oppressed, to all who suffered from the tyranny of men or of Satan ; it yearned with unspeakable tenderness over the perishing and the degraded, it cherished with warmest kindliness all the true children of God.

And love repaid him—a love which could take pleasure in the very roughnesses of his genius, the knots and excres cences of a character grandly rugged like a wide-spreading British oak, which found a sort of fascination in the home-spun plainness that shocked super-sensitive refinement, but that well beseemed this 'son of the soil,' called, like Elisha, from his plough to speak the Word of God. The simple, unconscious heroism of his life, wholly ruled by loving, self-renouncing duty, was only made fully known after his death; and the revelation endeared him the more to those who prized his worth. They learned without surprise how, when the quarterly instalments of his slender income were made over to him, he would say to the friend entrusted with the payment, 'I want you to take £10 of this for the missions, I have no use for the whole,' and how, the unconventional proposal being refused, he found other ways of devoting no small part of his modest savings to the cause he loved, as well as to funds which appealed to him because they bene-fited the ministers of the Church to which he had attached himself with full conviction. That he should give freely of his little worldly wealth was a small matter compared with the gift of his life and all its powers that he had made ungrudgingly; but the one was in complete harmony with the other.

The powerful voice has long been silent, and the number of those on whose ear its echoes lingered is lessening con-tinually; we can only reproduce imperfectly some passages from the discourses, some snatches of the conversation, that once were instinct with such power; but the consecrated life may still be studied, the example may yet be imitated, as the impassioned eloquence of the preacher never could be.

May he have spoken yet once more in these pages by that noble example of Christ-like, unselfish devotion; may the spectacle of his unfaltering faith rekindle dying faith; may those lingering echoes of his pleading, winning, cheering accents reach some hearts that need a voice like his to awaken and encourage them !

For the Gospel which he lived to proclaim is ever new and ever true and ever needed ; and in his own life it may be seen fairly written — not 'blotted and blurred with sin, but traced by the finger of God ; worthy to be read of all men—to be posted at the corner of every street—to be read in time, and in eternity.'

With these simple, glowing words in which he spoke the praise of some other saints of God, we take our leave, for the moment, of William Dawson.

HAYMAN, CHRISTY & LILLY, LTD., 113, FARRINGDON ROAD, LONDON, E.C.

The Gospel of Righteousness; or, Short Studies, Homiletical and Expository, on the Sermon on the Mount. By Rev. JOHN HARRIES, Author of 'Does God Break His Pledges?' 'The Saving Spirit,' etc. With an Introduction by Rev. James Chapman. Crown 8vo. 2s. 6d.

Naaman the Syrian, and Other Sermons preached at St. James's Hall. By MARK GUY PEARSE. Royal 16mo. Red lines round page. 2s. 6d.

Christianity and Socialism. By Rev. WILLIAM NICHOLAS, M.A, D.D. The Fernley Lecture of 1893. Demy 8vo. Paper Covers 2s.; cloth 3s.

The Mulchester Muddle. A Story. By FRIBA, Author of 'Miss Kennedy and Her Brothers,' 'The Two Cousins,' etc., etc. Crown 8vo. 2s. 6d.

Amos Truelove. By CHARLES R. PARSONS. Crown 8vo. Illustrated. Cloth, 1s. 6d., gilt edges. 2s. 6d.

Rev. Alexander McAulay as I Knew Him. By WILLIAM SAMPSON. Illustrated. Crown 8vo. Gilt edges. 2s.

Hawthornvale. By Rev. JAMES CUTHBERTSON. Crown 8vo. Illustrated. 2s.

The Star in the East. A Story. By RICHARD ROWE, Author of 'Diary of an Early Methodist,' 'Famous British Explorers,' etc. Crown 8vo. Illustrated. 1s. 6d.

Strange Life Stories. By CHARLES R. PARSONS, Author of 'The Man with the White Hat,' 'Vicar of Berrybridge,' 'Amos Truelove,' etc., etc. Crown 8vo. Numerous Illustrations. 1s. 6d.

The Hand on the Helm. By Rev. F. A. TROTTER. Crown 8vo. Illustrated. 1s. 6d.

Missionary Veterans in South Africa. Sketches of the Lives, Labours, and Triumphs of Barnabas Shaw, T. L. Hodgson, and John Edwards. By Rev. J. MARRAT. Crown 8vo. Illustrated. 1s. 6d.

The Soldiers of Liberty. A Story of the Siege of Leyden. By EMILY P. WEAVER, Author of 'The Rabbi's Sons.' Crown 8vo. Illustrated. 1s. 6d.

Children of the Court, and Two Little Waifs. By F. M. HOLMES. Crown 8vo. Illlustrated 1s. 6d.

Sybil's Repentance. By Mrs. M. S. HAYCRAFT, Author of 'The New Headmaster,' 'Springtide Reciter,' etc. Crown 8vo. Frontispiece. 1s. 6d.

Jacob Winterton's Inheritance. By EMILIE SEARCHFIELD, Author of 'Those Watchful Eyes,' etc. Crown 8vo. Frontispiece. 1s. 6d.

John Nelson, Mason and Missionary in the Heathen England of the Eighteenth Century. By ANNE E. KEELING. Crown 8vo. Illustrated. 1s. 6d.

William Dawson; the Yorkshire Farmer and Eloquent Preacher. By ANNE E. KEELING. Illustrated. Crown 8vo, 1s. 6d.

London: C. H. KELLY, 2, Castle Street, City Road, E.C.;

AND 66, PATERNOSTER ROW, E.C.

𝕭ooks for 𝕭ible 𝕾tudents.

EDITOR: REV. ARTHUR E. GREGORY.

The Epistles of Paul the Apostle. A Sketch of their Origin
and Contents. By GEORGE G. FINDLAY, B.A., Tutor in Biblical Literature
and Exegesis, Headingley College. Small Crown 8vo. 2s. 6d. *Fourth
Thousand.*

> THE SCOTSMAN says: 'The reader will find here compressed into
> a small space what he must otherwise seek through many volumes. . . .
> Mr. Findlay has before now proved himself an able and accomplished ex-
> positor of St. Paul, and this little work will fully maintain his character.'

The Theological Student. A Handbook of Elementary
Theology. By J. ROBINSON GREGORY. 2s. 6d. *Third Thousand.* A full
List of Questions for Self-Examination, and an Explanatory Index of Theo-
logical Terms add greatly to the practical value of the book.

> Rev. Professor MARSHALL RANDLES, D.D., says: 'It is admir-
> ably adapted to meet the wants of candidates for the ministry and of many
> already in its ranks, as well as of the great body of Local Preachers.
> Without claiming for itself the more than doubtful virtue of superseding
> old theology by new, this volume presents the old with a cogency of
> argument and a vigour of expression sufficient to save even the ordinary
> reader from the sense of tediousness.'

The Gospel of St. John. An Exposition, with Short Notes.
By THOS. F. LOCKYER, B.A., Author of Expositions of the Epistle to the
Romans and the Epistle of James in *The Pulpit Commentary*. *Second
Thousand.* Small Crown 8vo. 2s. 6d.

> Rev. ALEXANDER MACLAREN, D.D, Manchester, writes: 'Of
> the careful study and devout sympathy with the deep things of John's
> Gospel which mark it. It seems to me an admirable condensed guide to
> its trend of thought, and I congratulate you on having done so difficult a
> thing so well.'

The Praises of Israel. An Introduction to the Study of
the Psalms. By W. T. DAVISON, M.A., D.D., Tutor in Systematic Theology,
Handsworth College, Birmingham. *Second Thousand*. Small Crown 8vo.
2s. 6d.

> Dr. MARCUS DODS writes: 'As nearly perfect as a manual can be.
> It is the work of a reverent and open-minded scholar, who has spared no
> pains to compress into this small volume the best information and the most
> trustworthy results arrived at by himself and other experts.'

From Malachi to Matthew. Outlines of the History of
Judea from 440 to 4 B.C. By R. WADDY MOSS, Tutor in Classics and
Mathematics, Didsbury College, Manchester. Small crown 8vo, 2s. 6d.

> 'Mr. Moss's book is worthy of the series. His style is straightforward
> and graphic. He can tell a story rapidly and forcibly. There is vigour
> and there is vitality throughout. It is to be hoped that these Manuals will
> be largely used.'—*The British Weekly.*

An Introduction to the Study of Hebrew. By J. T. L.
MAGGS, B.A, Prizeman in Hebrew and New Testament Greek, London
University. Small Crown 8vo, 5s.

> 'Mr. Maggs has done an excellent piece of useful, unpretending work.
> Its distinctive merit is the perfect clearness of its grammatical instruction.
> . . . . Mr. Maggs has certainly acquired a full appreciation of the points
> that at the outset require to be made clear.'—*The Literary World.*

In the Apostolic Age: The Churches and the Doctrine.
By Rev. R. A. WATSON, D.D. Small Crown 8vo, 2s. 6d.

London: C. H. KELLY, 2, Castle Street, City Road, E.C.;
AND 66, PATERNOSTER ROW. E.C.

3

The 'Life Indeed' Series.

Crown 8vo, price 3s. 6d. each Volume. First and Second Volumes now ready.

The Holy Spirit and Christian Privilege. By Rev. T. G. SELBY, Author of 'The Imperfect Angel' and 'The Lesson of a Dilemma.'

The Inspirations of the Christian Life. By Rev. T. F. LOCKYER, B.A., Author of 'The Gospel of St. John : An Exposition.'

IN PREPARATION.

The Discipline of the Soul: Its Aims and Methods. By Prof. R. WADDY MOSS, Author of 'From Malachi to Matthew.'

The Laws of Spiritual Growth. By Rev. H. J. PIGGOTT, B.A.

The Origin of the Christian Life. By Rev. E. E. JENKINS, LL.D., Author of 'My Sources of Strength,' etc.

The Life Indeed. By Rev. W. L. WATKINSON, Author of 'The Influence of Scepticism on Character,' 'The Beginning of the Christian Life,' etc.

Copyright Editions of Popular American Authors.

The Gilead Guards: A Story of the American Civil War. By Mrs. O. W. SCOTT. Illustrated. Crown 8vo, 2s. 6d.

Ringing Bells. By REESE ROCKWELL, Author of 'Grand Gilmore.' Illustrated. Crown 8vo, 2s. 6d.

'Wanted.' By PANSY. Illustrated. Crown 8vo, 2s. 6d.

Stephen Mitchell's Journey. By PANSY. Crown 8vo. Frontispiece. 2s. 6d.

'Has all the graceful simplicity, earnest purpose, and practical godliness which are so characteristic of Mrs. Alden's writings.'—*The Christian.*

Twenty Minutes Late. By PANSY. Crown 8vo. Frontispiece. 2s. 6d.

'Pansy is the author of some of the brightest and best story books which have been issued in recent years. "Twenty Minutes Late" is a particularly lively and well illustrated piece of healthy fiction.'—*Lincolnshire Free Press.*

London: C. H. KELLY, 2, Castle Street, City Road, E.C.;

AND 66, PATERNOSTER ROW, E.C.

4

John Remington, Martyr. By PANSY. A Sequel to
'Aunt Hannah and Martha and John.' Crown 8vo. Frontispiece. 2s. 6d.
    'This is, without exception, the best temperance story we have read for
a long time. The teaching is pronounced, thoroughly up to date, clear and
outspoken on every phase of the question.'—*The Western Temperance
Herald.*

Her Associate Members. By PANSY. Crown 8vo.
Frontispiece. 2s. 6d.
    'As a story writer we consider Pansy to be a specialist. For gentle
and simple, gracious and graceless, each and all, here is a bright and
beautiful book.'—*Sword and Trowel.*

Miss Dee Dunmore Bryant. By PANSY. Crown 8vo.
With Frontispiece. 2s. 6d.
    'We have no hesitation in saying that with each new volume Pansy excels
herself. "Aunt Hannah and Martha and John" pleased us more than any
other of her writings; but the book now before us pleases us most. It is
touchingly simple. . . . We trust that this book may prove a delight to
many children.'—*Methodist Recorder.*

Aunt Hannah and Martha and John. By PANSY and
Mrs. C. M. LIVINGSTONE. Crown 8vo. 2s. 6d.
    'Both cheap and good ; . . . . written with skill and ability, and in the
interest of truth and righteousness.'—*Primitive Methodist Magazine.*

Judge Burnham's Daughters. A Sequel to 'Ruth
Erskine's Crosses.' By PANSY. Crown 8vo. 2s. 6d.
    'A book of pearls, and the lover of religious truth will be thankful for it.'
—*Hastings and St. Leonard's Chronicle.*

Eighty-Seven : A Chautauqua Story. By PANSY. Crown
8vo. 2s.
    'There is a bracing tone about the book which seems to stir one up to
make better use of life's opportunities.'—*London Quarterly Review.*

A Modern Exodus. By FAYE HUNTINGTON. Author of
'Those Boys,' etc., etc. Crown 8vo. 2s. 6d.
    'Charmingly written, full of pathos, adventure, and exciting interest.'—
Newcastle Chronicle.

The Rabbi's Sons : A Story of the Days of St. Paul. By
EMILY P. WEAVER. Crown 8vo. Frontispiece. 2s. 6d.
    'Admirably calculated to familiarise the reader with the life and manners
of the Hebrews in the Early Christian era. The subject is as instructive
as the story is pleasant.'—*Birmingham Daily Gazette.*

Soldiers of Liberty : A Story of the Siege of Leyden. By
EMILY P. WEAVER Crown 8vo. Illustrated. 1s. 6d.
    'A more than ordinarily vigorous and enchanting Netherland story.'—
Lincolnshire Free Press.

London: C. H. KELLY, 2, Castle Street, City Road, E.C.;

AND 66, PATERNOSTER ROW E.C.

Cheap Editions of Popular Religious Books.

In Crown 8vo, cloth, gilt ettered, 1s. 6d.

William Dawson, the Yorkshire Farmer and Eloquent Preacher. By A. E. KEELING. Illustrated.

John Nelson, Mason and Mission- ary in the Heathen England of the Eighteenth Century. By A. E. KEELING. Illustrated.

Little Abe ; or, The Bishop of Berrybrow. Being the Life of Abraham Lockwood, a quaint and popular Yorkshire Local-Preacher. By F. JEWELL. Illustrated. *Eighteenth Thousand.*

The Backwoods Preacher. Being the Autobiography of Peter Cartwright, an American Methodist Travelling Preacher. *Twenty-Second Thousand.*

The Village Blacksmith ; or, The Life of Samuel Hick. By JAMES EVERETT. *Forty-Eighth Thousand.*

John Wesley: His Life and His Work. By Rev. M. LELIEVRE, D.D.

Reminiscences of Isaac Marsden, of Doncaster. By JOHN TAYLOR. *Eighth Thousand.*

The Apostles of Fylde Methodism. By JOHN TAYLOR. Three Portraits and Map.

The Tongue of Fire ; or, The True Power of Christianity. By Rev. W. ARTHUR, M.A.

Lessons of Prosperity; and other Addresses delivered at Noon-Day in the Philosophical Hall, Leeds. By Rev. W. L. WATKINSON. *Third Thousand.*

Mistaken Signs ; and other Papers on Christian Life and Experience. *Fifth Thousand.* By Rev. W. L. WATKINSON.

Noon-day Addresses delivered in the Central Hall, Manchester. By W. L. WATKINSON. *Sixth Thousand.*

Loving Counsels : Sermons and Addresses. By Rev. CHARLES GARRETT. *Fourteenth Thousand.*

John Nelson's Journal.

The Marrow of Methodism. Twelve Sermons by J. WESLEY. With Introduction and Analysis by Dr. GREGORY.

The Man with the White Hat ; or, The Story of an Unknown Mission. By C. R. PARSONS. Twenty-one Illustrations. *Twentieth Thousand.*

The Vicar of Berrybridge. By C. R. PARSONS. *Eighth Thousand.* Thirty-seven Illustrations.

Roger Wentwood's Bible. By C. R. PARSONS. Nineteen Illustrations.

Amos Truelove. By C. R. PARSONS. 26 Illustrations.

Leaves from My Log of Twenty- five Years Work amongst Sailors and others in the Port of London. By T. C. GARLAND. Illustrated. *Tenth Thousand.*

East End Pictures ; or, More Leaves from My Log. By T. C. GARLAND. Illustrated. *Sixth Thousand.*

Elias Power of Ease-in-Zion. By Rev. J. M. BAMFORD. Illustrated. *Twentieth Thousand.*

John Conscience, of Kingseal. By Rev. J. M. BAMFORD. Illustrated. *Ninth Thousand.*

Father Fervent. By Rev. J. M. BAMFORD. Illustrated. *Sixth Thousand.*

Hugh Axe, of Hephzibah. By Rev. J. M. BAMFORD. Illustrated. *Third Thousand.*

London: C. H. KELLY, 2, Castle Street, City Road, E.C.;
AND 66, PATERNOSTER ROW, E.C.

By the Rev. W. L. Watkinson.

Lessons of Prosperity; and other Addresses Delivered at Noon-Day in the Philosophical Hall, Leeds. *Third Thousand.* Crown 8vo. Paper covers, 1s.; cloth, 1s. 6d.

Noon-Day Addresses delivered in the Central Hall, Manchester. *Sixth Thousand.* Crn. 8vo. Paper covers, 1s.; cloth, 1s. 6d.

Mistaken Signs; and other Papers on Christian Life and Experience. *Fifth Thousand.* Crn. 8vo. Paper covers, 1s.; cloth, 1s. 6d.

The Influence of Scepticism on Character. *Eighth Thousand.* The Fernley Lecture of 1886. Demy 8vo. Paper covers, 1s. 6d.; cloth, 2s. 6d.

John Wicklif. *Second Thousand.* With Portrait and Eleven other Illustrations. Crown 8vo. 2s. 6d.

The Beginning of the Christian Life. *Sixth Thousand.* 16mo. 1s.

The Programme of Life. *Fifth Thousand.* Demy 16mo. 1s.

By the Rev. John M. Bamford.

Christ in the City: a Series of Meditations. Companion Volume to 'My Cross and Thine.' Crown 8vo. Red lines round page. Cloth, red edges. 3s.

My Cross and Thine. Large Crown 8vo. Red lines round pages. Ten full page Illustrations. Cloth, red edges. 3s. 6d.

Hugh Axo, of Hephzibah. Crown 8vo. Six Page Illustrations, 1s. 6d.; gilt edges, 2s.

Father Fervent. *Sixth Thousand.* Crown 8vo. Eighteen Illustrations, 1s. 6d.; gilt edges, 2s. 6d.

A Week of Life. Small Crn. 8vo. With Frontispiece, cloth, 6d.

Elias Power, of Ease in Zion. *Twentieth Thousand.* Crn. 8vo. Seventeen Illustrations, 1s. 6d.; gilt edges, 2s. 6d.

John Conscience, of Kingseal. *Ninth Thousand.* Crn. 8vo. Eighteen Illustrations, 1s. 6d.; gilt edges, 2s. 6d.

The Cracked Hearthstone. Crn. 8vo. Illus., 2s.; gilt edges, 2s. 6d.

By Charles R. Parsons.

Amos Truelove. Crown 8vo. Illustrated, 1s. 6d; gilt edges, 2s. 6d.

The Vicar of Berrybridge. Crn. 8vo. Thirty-seven Illustrations. *Eighth Thousand.* Paper covers, 1s.; cloth, 1s. 6d.; gilt edges, 2s. 6d.

The Man with the White Hat; or, The Story of an Unknown Mission. 21 Illustrations. *Twentieth Thousand.* Crn. 8vo. Paper covers, 1s.; cloth, 1s. 6d.; gilt edges, 2s. 6d.

Roger Wentwood's Bible. Crown 8vo. Numerous Illustrations, 1s. 6d.; gilt edges, 2s. 6d.

Purity and Power. Crown 8vo. Cloth, red edges, 2s. 6d.

Strange Life Stories. Numerous Illustrations. Crown 8vo. 1s. 6d.

Farmer Read's Kingdom; the Story of One Poplar Farm. Eighteen Illustrations. Crown 8vo. 1s. 6d.

The Little Woman in Grey; Scenes and Incidents in Home Mission Work. Twenty-two Illustrations. Crown 8vo. 2s. 6d.

By Evelyn Everett-Green.

Miss Meyrick's Niece, Illustrated. Crown 8vo. 2s.

My Black Sheep. Illustrated. Crown 8vo. 2s.

London: C. H. KELLY, 2, Castle Street, City Road, E.C.;
AND 66, PATERNOSTER ROW, E.C.

By Ruth Elliott.

Fought and Won. A Story of Grammar School Life. *Fifth Thousand.* Crown 8vo. Frontispiece, 2s. 6d.

'Twixt Promise and Vow; and other Stories. *Second Thousand.* Crown 8vo. Frontispiece, 1s. 6d.

Auriel, and other Tales. *Third Thousand.* Crown 8vo. Frontispiece, 1s. 6d.

John Lyon; or, From the Depths. *Ninth Thousand.* Crm. 8vo. Five Illustrations, 3s. 6d.

Undeceived; Roman or Anglican? A Story of English Ritualism. *Ninth Thousand.* Crm. 8vo. 2s. 6d.

James Daryll; or, From Honest Doubt to Christian Faith. *Ninth Thousand.* Crown 8vo. 2s.

A Voice from the Sea; or, The Wreck of the 'Eglantine.' *Sixth Thousand.* Crown 8vo. 1s. 6d

Little Ray and her Friends. Illustrated. *Seventh Thousand.* Royal 16mo. 1s. 4d.

Talks with the Bairns about Bairns. Illustrated. *Second Thousand.* Royal 16mo. 1s. 4d.

My First Class, and other Stories. Illustrated. *Second Thousand.* Royal 16mo. 1s. 4d.

Margery's Christmas-Box. Seven Illustrations. Royal 16mo. 9d.

By Anne E. Keeling.

Heroines of Faith and Charity. Crown 8vo. 11 Illustrations, 2s. 6d.; cloth, gilt edges, 3s.

Eminent Methodist Women. Cr. 8vo. With Four Portraits on Steel, 2s. 6d.; cloth, gilt edges, 3s.

The Nine Famous Crusades of the Middle Ages. Crown 8vo. Numerous Illustrations, 2s. 6d.

John Nelson, Mason and Mission- ary in the Heathen England of the Eighteenth Century. Illustrated. Crown 8vo. 1s. 6d.

Great Britain and Her Queen. A Summary of Events of Her Reign. Crown 8vo. Profusely Illustrated with Portraits of Men of the Period, 1s. 6d.; cloth, gilt edges, 2s.

Andrew Golding; A Story of the Great Plague. 3 Illus. Crn 8vo. 2s.

The Pride of the Family. Illustrated. Second Edit. Crn. 8vo. 2s.

General Gordon: Hero and Saint. Illustrated. Crown 8vo. 2s. 6d.

The Oakhurst Chronicles: A Tale of the Times of Wesley. Five Illustrations. Crown 8vo. 2s.

Castle Malling: A Yorkshire Story. Crown 8vo. Six Illustrations. 2s.

William Dawson, the Yorkshire Farmer and Eloquent Preacher. Illustrated. Crown 8vo. 1s. 6d.

Bernard Palissy, the Huguenot Potter. Small Crown 8vo, cloth, 6d.; gilt edges, 8d.

The Wren's Nest at Wrenthorpe. Imperial 32mo. Cloth, 6d.; cloth, gilt lettered, 8d.

'Helps Heavenward.'

The Beginning of the Christian Life. By Rev. W. L. WATKINSON, *Sixth Thousand.* 16mo. 1s.

The Programme of Life. By Rev. W. L. WATKINSON. *Fifth Thousand.* 16mo. 1s.

God and Nature. By Rev. N. CURNOCK, F.R.M.S. *Third Thousand.* 16mo. 1s.

Christian Childhood. By Rev. A. E. GREGORY. *Third Thousand.* 16mo. 1s.

The Word in the Heart. Notes on the Devotional Study of Holy Scripture. By Rev. W. T. DAVISON, M.A. *Sixth Thousand.* 16mo. 1s.

The Coming of the King. Thoughts on the Second Advent. By Rev. J. ROBINSON GREGORY. *Second Thousand.* 16mo. 1s.

London: C. H. KELLY, 2, Castle Street, City Road, E.C.;
AND 66, PATERNOSTER ROW, E.C.

By Helen Briston.

Shadows: How they Came and Went. Crown 8vo. Illustrated. 2s. 6d.

Vaughan Persey. Crown 8vo. Illustrated. 2s. 6d.

May's Captain. Crown 8vo. Illustrated. 1s. 6d.

Beatrice and Brian. Small Crown 8vo. Illustrated. 1s.

The Poor Boy of the Class. Small Crown 8vo. Illustrated. 1s.

Tell Me a Story: Yes, I Will. Small Crown 8vo. Illustrated. 1s.

By M. S. Haycraft.

Sybil's Repentance; or, A Dream of Good. Crown 8vo. Illustrated. 1s. 6d.

The New Headmaster; or, Little Speedwell's Victory. Crown 8vo. Frontispiece 1s. 6d.

Brookside School, and Other Stories. Small Crown 8vo. Illustrated 1s.

The Springtide Reciter. A Book for Band of Hope Meetings. Small Crown 8vo. Illustrated. 1s.

Open Flowers, and Other Stories. Small Crown 8vo. Illustrated. 9d.

A Posy of Pinks, and Other Stories. Small Crown 8vo. Illustrated, 6d.

By Nellie Cornwall.

Mad Margrete and Little Gunnvald. A Norwegian Story. Illustrated. Crown 8vo. 2s. 6d.

Sprattie and the Dwarf; or The Shining Stairway. A Story of East London. Second Thousand. Crown 8vo. Illustrated. 2s.

Grannie Tresawnas' Story. Crown 8vo. Third Thousand. Frontispiece. 2s.

Daddy Longlegs and His White Heath Flower. Small Crown 8vo. Illustrated. 6d. Gilt Edges, 8d.

Faithful Rigmor and Her Grandmother. Small Crown 8vo. Illustrated. 6d.

By Emilie Searchfield.

Jacob Winterton's Inheritance. Crown 8vo. Illustrated. 1s. 6d.

Nina's Burnished Gold. Crown 8vo. Frontispiece. 1s. 6d.

Those Watchful Eyes; or Jemmy and His Friends. Third Thousand. Crown 8vo. Illustrated. 1s. 6d.

Afterward. Fcap. 8vo. Illustrated. 1s.

Poppy's Life Service. Fcap. 8vo. Illustrated. 1s.

My Brother Jack. Small Crown 8vo. Illustrated. 1s.

Deborah's Trials and Triumphs. Small Crown 8vo. Illustrated. 6d.

By Kate T. Sizer.

Dickon o'Greenwood; or, How the Light came to Lady Clare. A Village Picture in Martyr Days. Crown 8vo. Illustrated. 2s.

Avice Tennant's Pilgrimage. A Story of Bunyan's Days. Third Thousand. Crown 8vo. Illustrated. 2s.

Ephraim Wragge's Recollections. Small Crown 8vo. Illustrated. 6d.

By Emma Leslie.

Lady Marjorie: A Story of Methodist Work a Hundred Years Ago. Crown 8vo. Illustrated. 2s. Gilt Edges, 2s. 6d.

Cecily: a Tale of the English Reformation. Third Thousand. Crown 8vo. Illustrated. 2s. 6d.

London: C. H. KELLY, 2, Castle Street, City Road, E.C.;
AND 66, PATERNOSTER ROW, E.C.

9

Price Three and Sixpence.

The Light of the World : Lessons from the Life of our Lord for Children. By the Rev. RICHARD NEWTON, D.D. Foolscap 4to. Numerous Illustrations. (May also be had with gilt edges, price 4s. 6d.)

By Canoo and Dog Train among the Cree and Salteaux Indians. By EGERTON R. YOUNG. *Fourteenth Thousand*. With Portraits of the Rev. E. R. and Mrs. Young, Map, and Thirty-two Illustrations.

Stories from Indian Wigwams and Northern Camp Fires. By E. R. YOUNG. Forty-three Illustrations.

Four Years in Upper Burma. By W. R. WINSTON. Imperial 16mo. Numerous Illustrations.

Marion West. By M. E. SHEPHERD. Crown 8vo. Five Illustrations. Gilt edges.

The Two Cousins. By FRIBA. Frontispiece. Crown 8vo.

Uncle Jonathan's Walks in and Around London. New and Enlarged Edition. Foolscap 4to. Profusely Illustrated. Cloth, gilt lettered. Gilt edges.

Our Sea-girt Isle : English Scenes and Scenery Delineated. By Rev. JABEZ MARRAT. 2nd Ed. Enlarged. 217 Ilus. and Map. Imp 16mo.

Pillars of Our Faith. A Study in Chr̶ ̶ ̶ ̶e. By R. P. Dov̶ ̶ ̶ ̶, L̶L̶.D̶. *Third Thousand*. Demy 8vo.

Price Three Shillings.

Heroines of Faith and Charity. By A. E. KEELING. Crown 8vo. Illustrated. Gilt edges.

Marion West. By MARY E. SHEPHERD. Crn. 8vo. Five Illus.

Eminent Methodist Women. By ANNE E. KEELING. Crown 8vo. With Four Portraits on Steel. Gilt edges.

Price Two and Sixpence.

The Man who Spelled the Music, and other Stories. By MARK GUY PEARSE. Crown 8vo. Illustrated. Gilt edges.

Lady Marjorie. A Story of Methodist Work a Hundred Years Ago. By EMMA LESLIE. Crown 8vo. Illustrated.

Shadows : How They Came and Went. By HELEN BRISTON. Crn. 8vo. Illustrated.

Vaughan Persey. By HELEN BRISTON. Crown 8vo. Illustrated.

A Tangled Yarn. Captain James Payen's Life Log. Edited by T. DURLEY. Crown 8vo. Portrait.

Nathanael Noble's Homely Talks for Years and Youth. By Rev. H. SMITH. Crown 8vo. Illustrated. Gilt edges.

The Mulchester Muddle. A Story. By FRIBA. Crown 8vo. Illustrated.

Eminent Methodist Women. By ANNE E. KEELING. Crown 8vo. With Four Portraits on Steel.

Heroines of Faith and Charity. By A. E. KEELING. Crown 8vo. Eleven Illustrations.

Uncle Jonathan's Walks in and Around London. New and Enlarged Edition. Foolscap 4to. Profusely Illustrated.

Famous British Explorers, from Drake to Franklin. By R. ROWE. Imperial 16mo. Illustrated.

Parson Hardwork's Nut, and How He Cracked It. By W. W. HAUGHTON. Crown 8vo. Illustrated. Gilt edges.

Father Fervent. By Rev. JOHN M. BAMFORD. *Sixth Thousand*. Crn. 8vo. Gilt edges. Illustrations.

Elias Power, of "Ease-in-Zion." By Rev. JOHN M. BAMFORD. *Twentieth Thousand*. Crown 8vo. Fifteen Illustrations. Gilt edges.

London : C. H. KELLY, 2, Castle Street, City Road, E.C. ;
AND 66, PATERNOSTER ROW, E.C.

Lightning Source UK Ltd.
Milton Keynes UK
UKHW010759211118
332624UK00007B/282/P